INTERNET

Home.P@ge.Design

INTERNET.Home.Page.Design

Edited by Hayashi Sakawa & Kazuhiro Hayase

© 1996 First Japanese edition published by Graphic-sha
Publishing Co. Ltd.

First German edition was published in 1997 by :
NIPPAN Verlag
Nippon Shuppan Hanbai Deutschland GmbH
Krefelder Strasse 85
D-40549 Duesseldorf, Germany
Phone : +49-211-5048080
Fax   : +49-211-5049326

ISBN3-910052-98-3

Printed in Hong Kong by Everbest Printing Co. Ltd.

First Printing, 1997

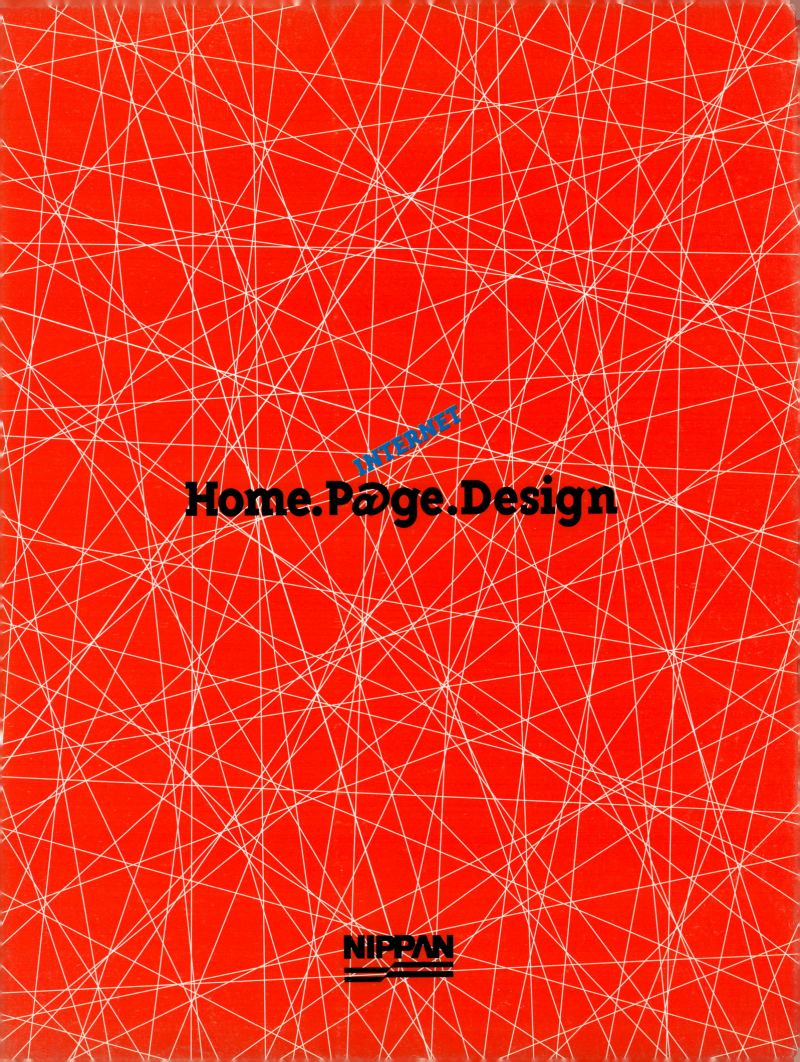

Home.P@ge.Design

INTERNET

NIPPAN

In Pursuit of Internet Design

by Mitsuo Katsui (Art Director)

Great changes in ordinary life seem to occur these days in a matter of months. Already, the word "multimedia" is hardly new; and, now, we can no longer pick up a newspaper or see a television program in which the Internet is not an important topic. It is a little belatedly, then, that we graphic designers are starting to set up our own homepages and do business over the Internet. It is a little late, too, that the six-thousand member Japan Industrial Design Promotion Organization has finally launched JIDPO Japan Design to build a communication network for the whole field. Nonetheless, interactive links are now growing so fast that the growth reminds me of human development. The well-known writer Takashi Tachibana says that the growth of the Internet communication network is similar to the multiplication of human brain cells through cell division. I fully agree. Like the brain cells of newborn babies, the nerve cells of the Internet are beginning to multiply, extending their hands to each other and growing into an ever more complicated network. Like children on the eve of their Coming-of-Age Day, the Internet is on the threshold of its adulthood.

Looking at the Internet from a global point of view, we can already see a new world of information different from the real world. Like an artist's canvas before the painting begins, the information space on the Internet is vast and has unlimited potential. In homepage design, the latest expression appears and is constantly updated all day every day. It is ever changing, and a brand new aesthetic is now being born. When we consider that it took our forefathers many centuries to reach the stage of using books as a medium of expression, the fast-paced change of today is astounding. Our heritage is, nevertheless, precious to us, and it clearly serves as the basis of our modern communication design.

Digital information space is much the same as design. The basics of editorial design is as important to us as ever. But, because the vast amount of information that flows on the Internet is not always linked, we must now create better digital space by fully utilizing the interactive sensibility that is the special quality of multimedia. In Japan now, the Internet is a field in which only a small number of designers are involved. The number of artists working with digital images, however, is steadily increasing and expected to continue to increase in the future.

This publication is a milestone. It is the first to introduce actual homepages created abroad. It contains one hundred works of art selected for their excellence by Mr. Kazuhiro Hayase. Hayase is a designer who became involved in homepage designs. Without doubt, this book will appeal to anyone interested in this new wave of expression, and, at the same time, it will serve as a fine guide for digital designers who want to expand their use of the Internet for communication.

Towards a More Creative Web

by Masahiro Ikuta / Kinotrope, Inc.

Recently, I have a number of heated discussions about whether or not the Internet is interesting or useful. Such debate, however, seems fruitless to me. I think that, rather than wasting time on abstract arguments, it would be better for people to find out for themselves and to, in any case, create their own attractive and useful homepages. Moreover, by direct involvement, people can get to feel the tremendous satisfaction of participating in a brand new, wide open computer culture.

The Internet is now growing in an astronomical rate and has great influence on all aspects of society. For example, as the Internet allows individuals and corporations to talk to each other directly, they cannot help but interact with each other more honestly. And, since the rate of change is dizzying, I think it is advisable for people to try to make the right decisions about what is immediately achievable and then try to achieve it. Wondering whether or not to make the attempt is the same as opportunity lost.

Business on the Internet is currently booming. Our offices has become a "contents provider", creating our own web site and designing many homepages for our clients. We are now receiving many more inquiries and commissions than we could have predicted last year. Clearly, the Internet has captured the attention of all kinds of corporations and organizations.

However, people are not impressed by unattractive or boring homepages, nor do they enjoy seeing advertisements that do no more than boast or brag about some company. It is rather unfortunate when people who are curious about and willing to access the world wide web end up disappointed to find homepages which lack creativity.

But it does not have to be like that. With a little ingenuity, even under limited conditions, people can use the Internet to produce high-quality, creative homepages, and companies can be committed to enhancing their productions by soliciting and heeding feedback from users. Happily, both individuals and companies are already using their ingenuity as you will see by browsing through this book.

To me, homepage designs are more interesting when created by people who are feeling the power of personal expression for the first time. So, I find personal homepages to be the most exciting. Still, among the web sites now in existence, there are few that are truly interesting. So, I would like to offer a few tips that might help.

For one thing, if you have friends who use the Internet creatively, encourage them to use linking to improve the quality of the web. This may sound simplistic, but creative homepages tend to be linked to other creative ones. Start the ball rolling and you can extend to find interesting homepages appearing with great frequency. Another tip, just for your own enjoyment, is to access web sites produced by college students. Perhaps because they have more time and fewer preconceived ideas than older people, they create many amusing sites. Check them and you will surely be led to one that really appeals to you.

This book is a collection of creative homepages from the Internet and WWW that focus on visual design. It is also a showcase for works of art that have been created during the last few years. Let it inspire you to participate in making the web culture as creative as possible. Nobody knows which direction the Internet will take in the future, but it will be fun to watch its development and see what kind of culture we create.

E-Mail: masa@kinotrope.co.jp

INTERNET HOME PAGE DESIGN CONTENTS

DESIGN: INDIVIDUAL

ONLINEEXHIBITION

COMPUTER-RELATED

APPAREL

Auto Maker

Introduction

If you find in this book inspiring design or appealing message, why don't you switch on your computer and start up your browser? It is always best to check something out with your own eyes. Some of the sites will be very different from what you expected, but in most of them, you will find sophisticated and well-designed homepages.

As a designer, I am involved in constructing web sites, and, with my partners, I design the contents for a number of them. I get a lot of e-mails every day from people in various fields, and from their letters, it seems to me that users from abroad are much more eloquent than those in Japan. There is no greater joy for a homepage designer like me than to receive such mails.

Why don't you imitate that behavior? When you surf the net and find great homepages, why don't you send an e-mail to the designer saying job well done? With these few simple words, you can convey your feeling and bring them joy. I think that this kind of simple message can lead to broader and better communication.

Hayashi Sakawa

INTERNET

Home.
P@ge.
Design

www.nasa.gov

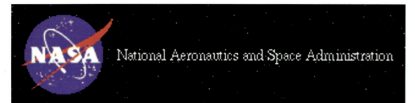

National Aeronautics and Space Administration

NASA

(http://www.nasa.gov)

National Aeronautics and Space Administration

Since the way to access NASA has already appeared in various Internet-related articles, you may have visited its site; however, aside from space fans or astronomy buffs, there is probably just a small number of people who have accessed it. Its vast amount of information is linked to and supplied by research institutes from across the U.S.A.

In fact, I accessed the site for the first time myself only after I began to compile this book. Its wide array of information about myriad fields at first overwhelmed me, but in the end, I gained a new understanding about many things. When you access NASA's homepage (www.nasa.gov), you will find a chic square-shaped graphic design with the intaglioed NASA symbol and color icons arranged against a quiet gray background. The icons are linked to each corner. This design serves as the basis for twelve corners linked to each button, but unfortunately, this style is only partially followed and a certain inconsistency between the corners results. This may have been inevitable, since the management of the homepage involved many designers.

What is most remarkable about this site is the reference photographs and videos, loaded into the gallery corner. it is truly wonderful that everyone has access to such valuable information and be able to look at the incredible space photographs taken by the Hubble telescope. Considering that, for the most part, this page was constructed by the technical staff and designers working in their spare time, it is amazing, both in quality and quantity. It becomes clear that, not only is freedom of information assured in the U.S. and people can keep a close watch over governmental and bureaucratic activities, but also that there is a vast extent of interactive designs.

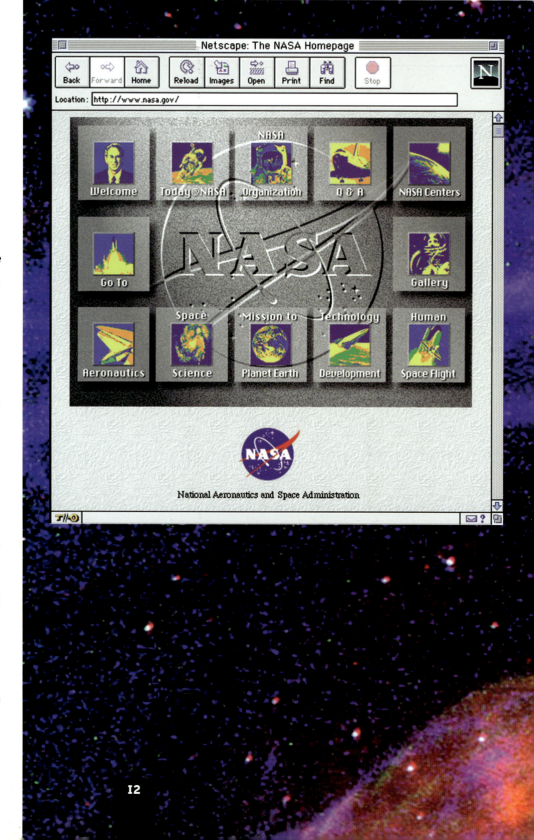

Back Forward Home Reload Images Open Print Find Stop

Location: http://www.nasa.gov/hqpao/apollo_11.html

Apollo 11

History

Mission Info

Mission Patch

Movies

Poster

NASA
Public Affairs

Images

Audio Files

NASA

National Aeronautics and Space Administration

This page covers the mission information from Apollo 11, the first spaceship in the history of mankind to land on the moon. We can access an array of videos, from the launching of the rocket to the landing on the moon, voices and sounds recorded during the satellite relay broadcasting may be heard.

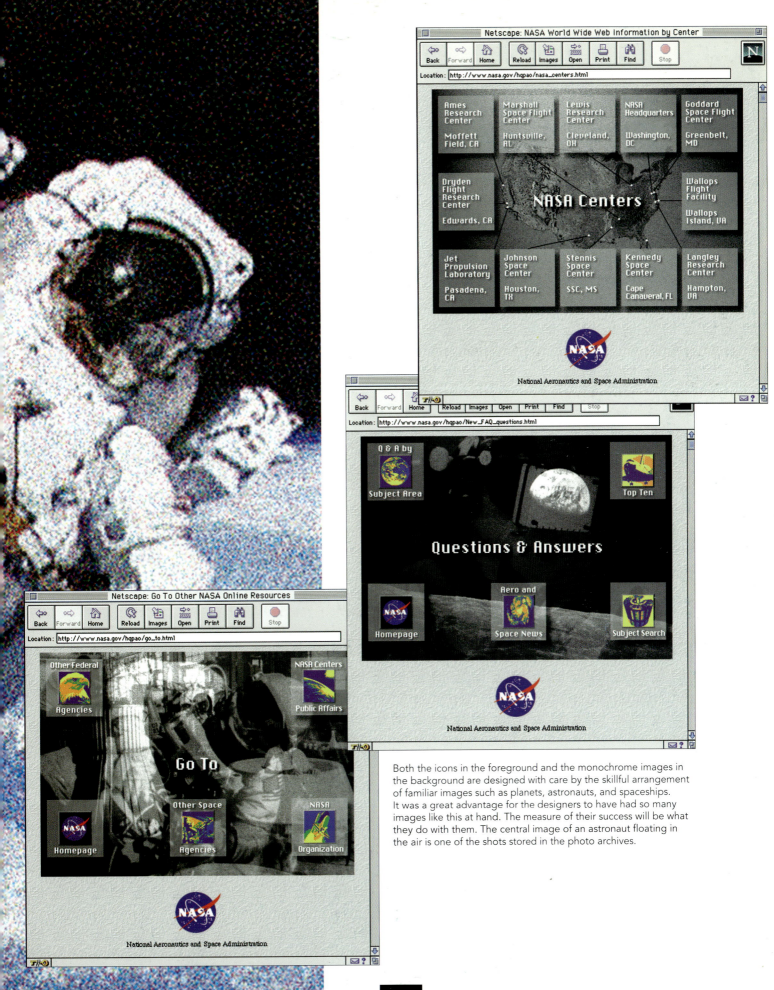

Netscape: NASA World Wide Web Information by Center

Location: http://www.nasa.gov/hqpao/nasa_centers.html

NASA Centers

- Ames Research Center — Moffett Field, CA
- Marshall Space Flight Center — Huntsville, AL
- Lewis Research Center — Cleveland, OH
- NASA Headquarters — Washington, DC
- Goddard Space Flight Center — Greenbelt, MD
- Dryden Flight Research Center — Edwards, CA
- Wallops Flight Facility — Wallops Island, VA
- Jet Propulsion Laboratory — Pasadena, CA
- Johnson Space Center — Houston, TX
- Stennis Space Center — SSC, MS
- Kennedy Space Center — Cape Canaveral, FL
- Langley Research Center — Hampton, VA

National Aeronautics and Space Administration

Netscape: (Questions & Answers)

Location: http://www.nasa.gov/hqpao/New_FAQ_questions.html

Questions & Answers

- Q & A by Subject Area
- Top Ten
- Homepage
- Aero and Space News
- Subject Search

National Aeronautics and Space Administration

Netscape: Go To Other NASA Online Resources

Location: http://www.nasa.gov/hqpao/go_to.html

Go To

- Other Federal Agencies
- NASA Centers / Public Affairs
- Homepage
- Other Space Agencies
- NASA Organization

National Aeronautics and Space Administration

Both the icons in the foreground and the monochrome images in the background are designed with care by the skillful arrangement of familiar images such as planets, astronauts, and spaceships. It was a great advantage for the designers to have had so many images like this at hand. The measure of their success will be what they do with them. The central image of an astronaut floating in the air is one of the shots stored in the photo archives.

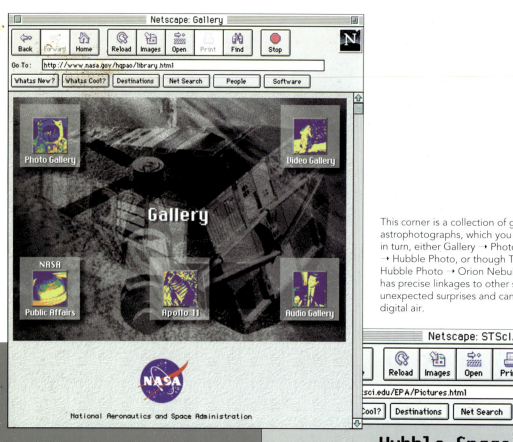

Netscape: Gallery

Back Forward Home Reload Images Open Print Find Stop

Go To: http://www.nasa.gov/hqpao/library.html

What is New? What is Cool? Destinations Net Search People Software

Photo Gallery

Video Gallery

Gallery

NASA
Public Affairs

Apollo 11

Audio Gallery

NASA

National Aeronautics and Space Administration

This corner is a collection of gorgeous astrophotographs, which you can get by selecting in turn, either Gallery → Photo Gallery → Telescope → Hubble Photo, or though Today's NASA → Hubble Photo → Orion Nebula. Since NASA's site has precise linkages to other sites, you will discover unexpected surprises and can enjoy a space walk in digital air.

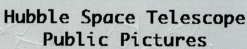

Netscape: STScI/HST Pictures

Reload Images Open Print Find Stop

...sci.edu/EPA/Pictures.html

...Cool? Destinations Net Search People Software

Hubble Space Telescope
Public Pictures

● Latest Release

● Pictures organized by subject
● 1996 Releases

● 1995 Releases

● HST's Greatest Hits 1990-1995 Picture Gallery

● 1994 Releases

● Comet/Jupiter Encounter
● Early Post-Servicing Mission (ERO) Images

● Pre-Servicing Mission Images

Note: Some of the above links contain thumbnail images which, though small, may take some time to transfer and display. You can reduce transfer times by setting an option in your browser, for example ''Delay Image Loading'' in the Options menu in Mosaic. There are some alternate links that do not include the thumbnails

Related Information

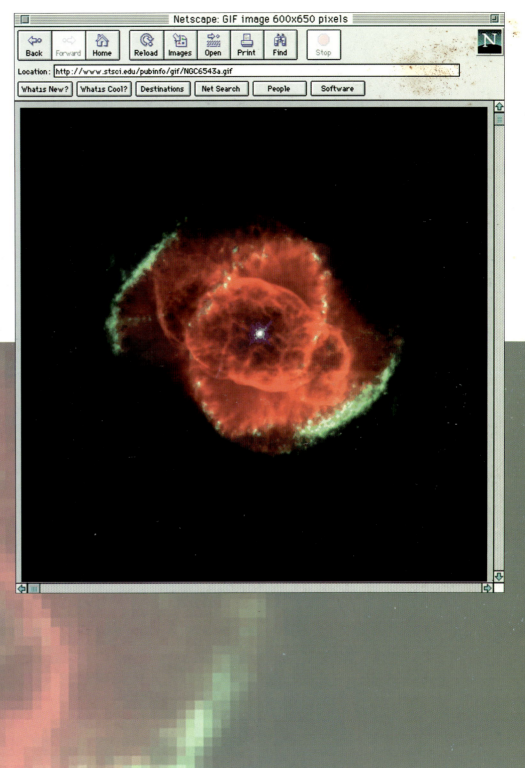

The photographic images taken by the Hubble telescope could never have been taken from earth. With one glance at these beautiful images, we can feel the vast extent and mystery of the space.

www.intac.com/~jdeck/ habib/index.html

TEEN SEXUALITY
in a culture of confusion

TEEN SEXUALITY

(http://www.intac.com/~jdeck/habib/index.html)

Design/Production Firm : Knox Turner Associates
Photo : Dan Habib
Design : Crankcase Multimedia

This homepage is submitted "In a culture of confusion" and is based on four years of detailed research by Dan Habib, a photo journalist. It shows his sincerity and his ability to turn a critical mind to the serious social problems facing teenagers.

The main characters appearing on this page are four teenagers of different races, nationalities, economic and social backgrounds, and sexual orientations. The detailed reports, which include their voices and are set against a neat black background, speak plainly about their real feelings, and their story develops smoothly. Shots of them taken during their ordinary daily life strengthens the visual impact of the story. Although this type of page deals with very serious material, the site is at once simple and impressive, and the sympathy of the designer for his subjects appeals to us greatly.

Teenagers face real emotional problems. By creating a page like this, Dan Habib shows both his sympathy for them and his desire to make their situation known. In addition to writing articles for a number of newspapers and magazines including *Time* and *Newsweek*, he has also won the Photographer of the Year award four times in New Hampshire.

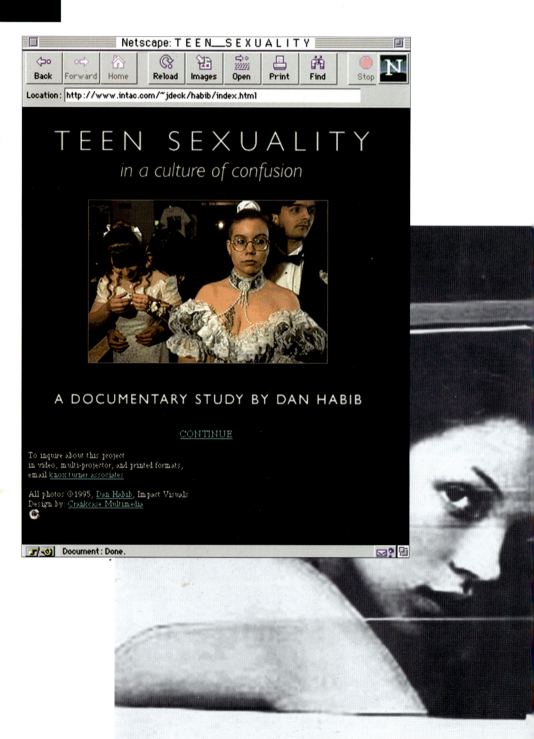

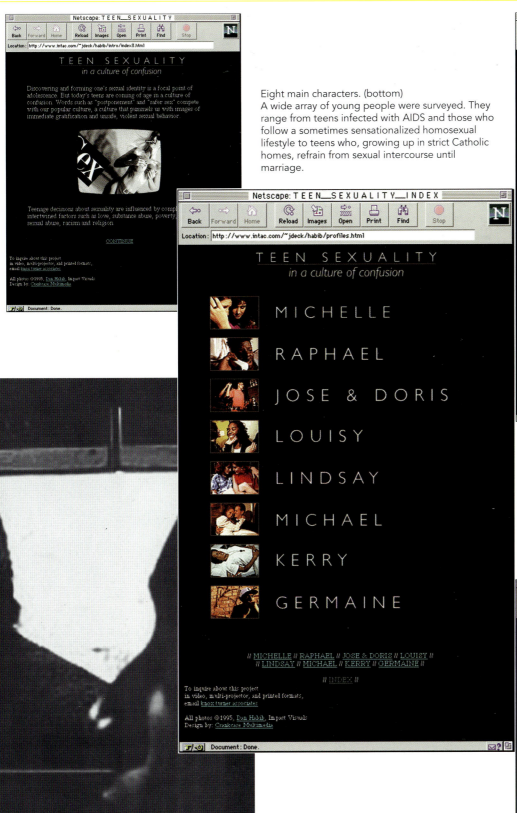

TEEN SEXUALITY
in a culture of confusion

Discovering and forming one's sexual identity is a focal point of adolescence. But today's teens are coming of age in a culture of confusion. Words such as "postponement" and "safer sex" compete with our popular culture, a culture that pummels us with images of immediate gratification and unsafe, violent sexual behavior.

Teenage decisions about sexuality are influenced by complex, intertwined factors such as love, substance abuse, poverty, sexual abuse, racism and religion.

CONTINUE

To inquire about this project
in video, multi-projector, and printed formats,
email knox turner associates

All photos ©1995, Don Habib, Impact Visuals
Design by: Crankcase Multimedia

Eight main characters. (bottom)
A wide array of young people were surveyed. They range from teens infected with AIDS and those who follow a sometimes sensationalized homosexual lifestyle to teens who, growing up in strict Catholic homes, refrain from sexual intercourse until marriage.

TEEN SEXUALITY
in a culture of confusion

MICHELLE

RAPHAEL

JOSE & DORIS

LOUISY

LINDSAY

MICHAEL

KERRY

GERMAINE

// MICHELLE // RAPHAEL // JOSE & DORIS // LOUISY //
// LINDSAY // MICHAEL // KERRY // GERMAINE //

// INDEX //

To inquire about this project
in video, multi-projector, and printed formats,
email knox turner associates

All photos ©1995, Don Habib, Impact Visuals
Design by: Crankcase Multimedia

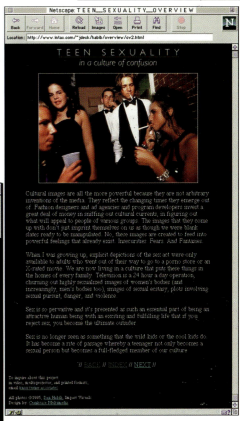

TEEN SEXUALITY
in a culture of confusion

Cultural images are all the more powerful because they are not arbitrary inventions of the media. They reflect the changing times they emerge out of. Fashion designers and ad agencies and program developers invest a great deal of money in sniffing out cultural currents, in figuring out what will appeal to people of various groups. The images that they come up with don't just imprint themselves on us as though we were blank slates ready to be manipulated. No, these images are created to feed into powerful feelings that already exist. Insecurities. Fears. And Fantasies.

When I was growing up, explicit depictions of the sex act were only available to adults who went out of their way to go to a porno store or an X-rated movie. We are now living in a culture that puts these things in the homes of every family. Television is a 24 hour a day operation, churning out highly sexualized images of women's bodies (and increasingly, men's bodies too), images of sexual ecstasy, plots involving sexual pursuit, danger, and violence.

Sex is so pervasive and it's presented as such an essential part of being an attractive human being with an exciting and fulfilling life that if you reject sex, you become the ultimate outsider.

Sex is no longer seen as something that the wild kids or the cool kids do. It has become a rite of passage whereby a teenager not only becomes a sexual person but becomes a full-fledged member of our culture.

// BACK // INDEX // NEXT //

To inquire about this project
in video, multi-projector, and printed formats,
email knox turner associates

All photos ©1995, Don Habib, Impact Visuals
Design by: Crankcase Multimedia

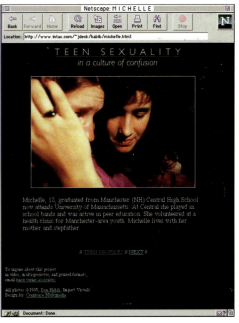

TEEN SEXUALITY
in a culture of confusion

Michelle, 18, graduated from Manchester (NH) Central High School now attends University of Massachusetts. At Central she played in school bands and was active in peer education. She volunteered at a health clinic for Manchester-area youth. Michelle lives with her mother and stepfather.

// TEEN PROFILES // NEXT //

To inquire about this project
in video, multi-projector, and printed formats,
email knox turner associates

All photos ©1995, Don Habib, Impact Visuals
Design by: Crankcase Multimedia

www-paradigm.asucla.ucla.edu/DB/DBHome/DBHome.html

Daily Bruin Online

(http://www-paradigm.asucla.ucla.edu/DB/DBHome/DBHome.html)

Design/Production Firm :
UCLA Electronic Mediacourse staff
Director : Laurel Davis
Assistant Director : Phillip Hong
Designer Director : Brenton Mar
Technical Director : Mark Arana

This is the online version of the UCLA students newspaper. Its homepage is better designed than that or many other students newspapers. How smart of the designers to incorporate advertisement into the site! What a clever way to raise the necessary funding! This kind of savvy may be influenced by the very nature of L.A., where the media is deeply rooted, or it may be due to the influence of UCLA itself.

The site is composed of various sections that introduce a number of musts for school life, including the following: daily news; an A&E column called Viewpoint; sports information; a section called Forums, where users can exchange opinions; a photo gallery; a Classifieds section; and a section where Back Issues can be found.

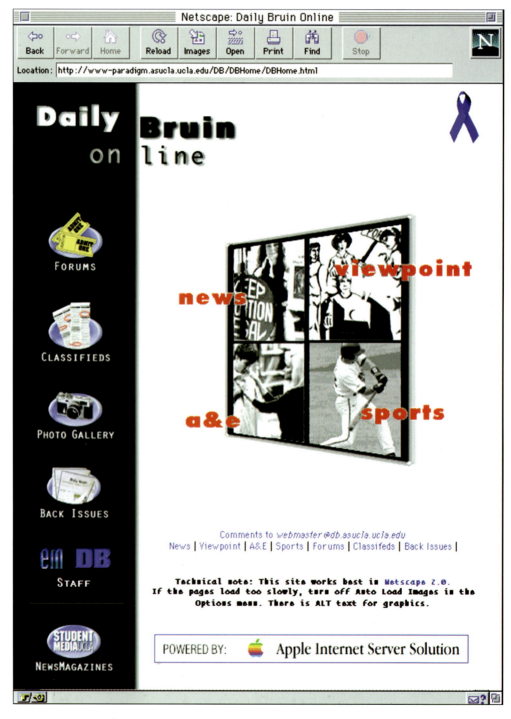

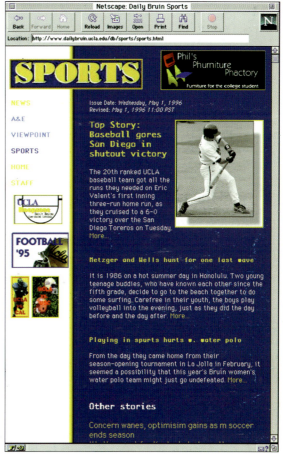

When we hear the name UCLA, we often think first of sports, because of their well-established basketball and football programs (top left), but the school has many excellent courses. Perhaps because it is located near Hollywood, the drama courses are a big draw, and many talented people have studied film there.

www.itp.tsoa.nyu.edu/ ~review

Review / ITP

(http://www.itp.tsoa.nyu.edu/~review)

Design/Production Firm :
Interactive Telecommunications
Program at NewYork University
Art Director/Designer : Lisa Natasha Cavender
Editor in Chief : Miles Kronby
Managing Editor : Jessica Safran
Senior Editor : Kevin Kanarek
New Media Editor : David Gusick

Review is a homepage created as part of various research and experiments of students at New York University. Its quality and quantity are well beyond the expertise of average college students. Pale colored graphics imposed on a mainly white, with just a little black, background create a unique and unified impression. The elements are not very large, but, designed skillfully and never obtrusive, they highlight the main critical text beautifully. Great technical and artistic skill is needed to replace graphic images with high-quality gradations containing GIF data, and these students show that skill. Much can be learned from the images found in this site.
The site has so many articles covering so many themes that it is impossible to go through it in a short time. But its atmosphere is not busy, and we can feel the urban elegance of New York City and the intelligent presence of NYU as a typical part of it.

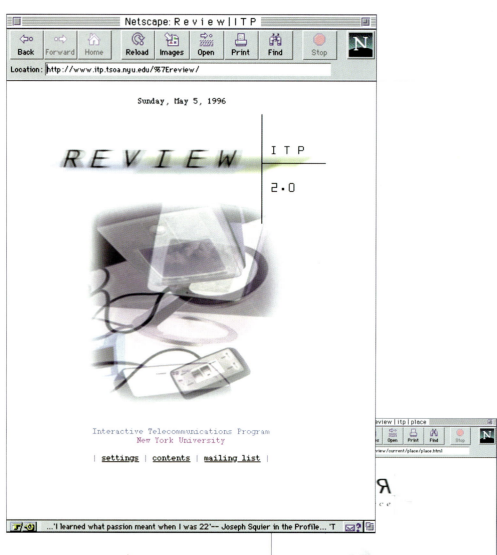

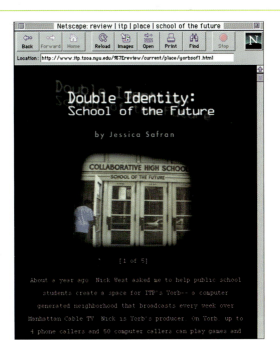

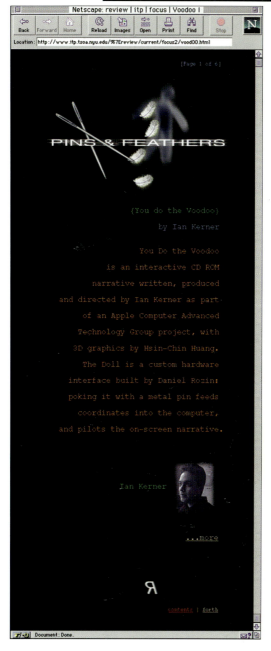

This menu page has an atmosphere similar to that of the title scroll screen of the film. (left) At our present technological stage, screens cannot be scroll automatically. How Exciting it will be when they can!

www.bbc.co.uk

BBC

(http://www.bbc.co.uk)
British Broadcasting Corp.

Design/Production : Firm BBC Networking Club
Client : BBC
Art Director : Dominik von Malaise
Creative Director : Julian Ellison
Copywriter : Emma Howard
Designer :
Dominik von Malaise,Chris Garcia
Illustrator : Norman Rosenberg
Photographer : BBC Library
HTML Writer :
Dominik von Malaise,Norman Rosenberg, Naomi Troski
Emma Howard,Julian Ellison,Chris Garcia,Gordon Joly
Programmer : Gordon Joly

Although the blue and white vertical rectangles of its background are often seen, I remember even now how impressed I was when I first saw it. The contents are divided into five corners. In Radio and Television, you can see the introduction of programs broadcasted through mass media; in Internet, you can see "one world online", with information gathered from its main information network. The site is constructed with an almost too neat visual design and seems to lack something, but BBC's intention is to present important information without ornamentation. The resultant graceful site all but compels us to examine BBC's thoughts carefully.

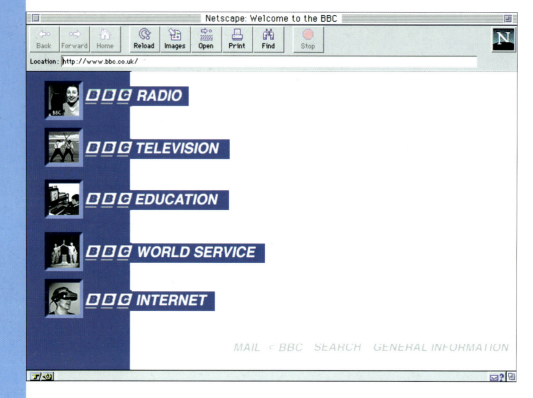

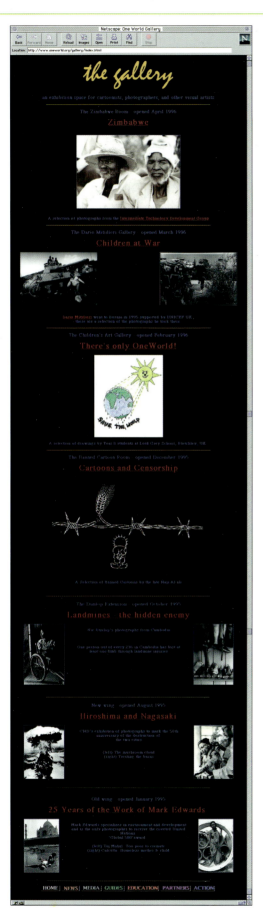

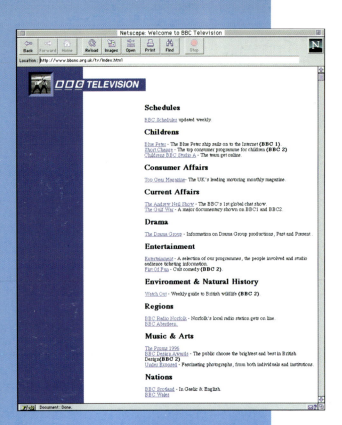

This design (top) is the prototype of BBC. It is up to the viewer to decide if it lacks something, but the screen clearly shows that the site holds a great deal of information.

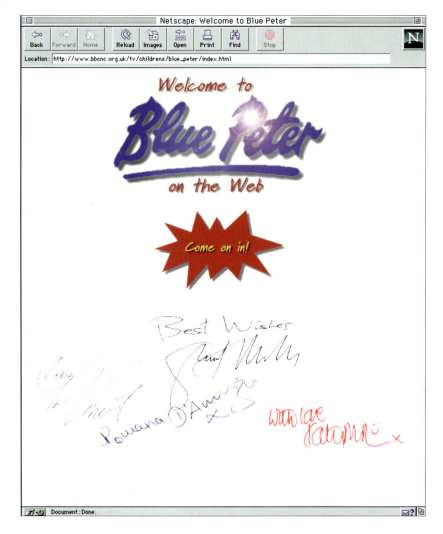

Back | Forward | Home | Reload | Images | Open | Print | Find | Stop

Location: http://www.bbcnc.org.uk/online/oneworld/top.html

Text Only Version Now Available

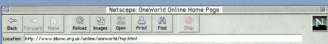
one world online

A MEETING PLACE FOR THE INTERNATIONAL COMMUNITY

Welcome
plus: how to join OneWorld

Those with fast Internet connections might enjoy a visit to the One World '96 Conference and Media Awards. The Conference debated impartiality in reporting, and the Awards featured the best in development and human rights broadcasting - all available in RealAudio and QuickTime video format.

🔍 **Search**

7.2 million
Total Accesses

NEWS | MEDIA | GUIDES | EDUCATION | PARTNERS | GALLERY | ACTION

Global news that really matters

ONE WORLD — NEWS

Christian Aid - IMF should sell gold to cancel poor country debt:
Why money flows from poor to rich -Top story, 3 May 1996
News from over 80 countries: Global themes and special reports from around the world [Image ©Christian Aid]

Your free online exhibition centre

ONE WORLD — GALLERY

Intermediate Technology in Zimbabwe: Photos from ITDG
The rest of the gallery: Landmines, banned cartoons, Hiroshima, the best of Mark Edwards' photos - plus art from Year 8 kids, UK. [Image ©ITDG]

Ways to get involved

ONE WORLD — ACTION

Appeal: Emergency appeal for relief in Lebanon - urgent request for funds from YMCA Care
The rest of the action: Feedback, jobs, voluntary work, conferences, diary and courses [Image ©TVE]

Broadcast, print, and new media

ONE WORLD — MEDIA

One World '96 Conference and Media Awards:
RealAudio of whole conference, video of best in broadcasting
The rest of the media pages: Television, books, radio, video-clips, CD-ROMs, videos, Internet links [Image ©BBC]

Your gateway to partners' own sites

ONE WORLD — PARTNERS

Save the Children's 'Poor in Health' report: Facts and case studies on the lack of healthcare in the majority world
All OneWorld's partner sites: Now 60-plus organisations - with their material regularly updated [Image ©SCF]

Resources for students and teachers

ONE WORLD — EDUCATION

The threat of poaching
Slaughter of last elephant in Zambian wildlife park
The rest of Y.E.S.: Youth diary, teacher training - and yards of classroom material [Image ©New Internationalist]

Guided tours of key OneWorld issues

ONE WORLD — GUIDES

Landmines Special Report: Regular updates from the Geneva Conference
The rest of the guides: On Bosnia, Rwanda, landmines, women's rights, refugees, cities and child rights [Image ©Pario Mitsikos]

 "Top 100 on the planet" - reviewers of 2ask

 Featured as Microsoft Network's 'Pick of the Week'

 "1995 Website of the Year" - Earthtimes

 "Top 5% of all WebSites" - Point

OneWorld Online is produced by the
One World Broadcasting Trust
a British charity linking the worlds of development and broadcasting.
Technical service provided by TECC.
OneWorld Online can also be found via the BBC's Web site

Earth satellite composite courtesy of Global Visions and University College London.

One World Online (top) is a page rich with information. At right is the *BBC Design Awards 1996*. Attractive images are used on this page, and, at bottom right, a typical web design, including a frame and moving images, can be seen the multimedia page.

Back | Forward | Home | Reload | Images | Open | Print | Find | Stop

Location: http://www.bbcnc.org.uk/tv/m&a/design_awards/index.html

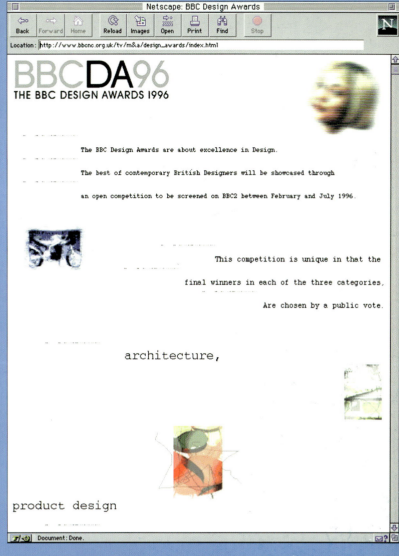

BBCDA96
THE BBC DESIGN AWARDS 1996

The BBC Design Awards are about excellence in Design.

The best of contemporary British Designers will be showcased through

an open competition to be screened on BBC2 between February and July 1996.

This competition is unique in that the

final winners in each of the three categories,

Are chosen by a public vote.

architecture,

product design

Document: Done.

Back | Forward | Home | Reload | Images | Open | Print | Find | Stop

Location: http://www.bbcnc.org.uk/the_centre/mmc.frames.html

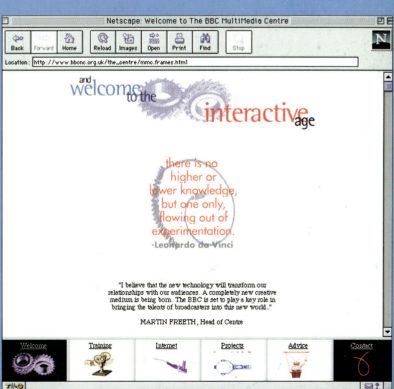

and welcome to the interactive age

there is no higher or lower knowledge, but one only, flowing out of experimentation.
-Leonardo da Vinci

"I believe that the new technology will transform our relationships with our audiences. A completely new creative medium is being born. The BBC is set to play a key role in bringing the talents of broadcasters into this new world."

MARTIN FREETH, Head of Centre

Welcome | Training | Internet | Projects | Advice | Contact

pathfinder.com/cgi-bin/ hbo/blackhistory

HBO CYBER SOUL CITY

HBO Cyber Soul City
(http://pathfinder.com/cgi-bin/hbo/blackhistory)

HBO (Home Box Office), one of the subsidiaries of the Time-Warner Group, is a provider of CATV programs. The homepage is also part of the Time Pathfinder site. Even though the word Harlem sometimes still carries a negative image, Harlem has, in fact, broken out of that image and has again become a center for events highlighting black culture as it was in the past. At the Cotton Club, for example, jazz has once again begun to thrive and so have intellectual and political movements propounding civil rights. HBO Cyber Soul City is an attractive homepage reminding us of the good old days. As you may guess from the title, you can get live information about the music, film, and sports of the area, where news stands, movie theaters, and barber shops abound. In particular, the barber shop corner is full of contemporary topics, such as boxing and entertainment, and its witty design reminds us that barber shops were once upon a time places for exchanging news, including even rumors and silly anecdotes, between fashionable gentlemen.

When the web boom began, it became so popular in Japan that many town, city, and shopping mall sites were constructed, but they incorporated mainly dull 3D images on their homepages. All of them had a stereotypical style and a prim air. But in HBO Cyber Soul City, the town has great charm because the streets are crowded with the comings and goings of the residents of the neighborhood, and they exude a kind of bawdy street culture. Modern buildings with a prim air are barely noticeable. The homepage is deliberately designed to have a low-tech look, while the contents are full of amazing devices. This site is great fun.

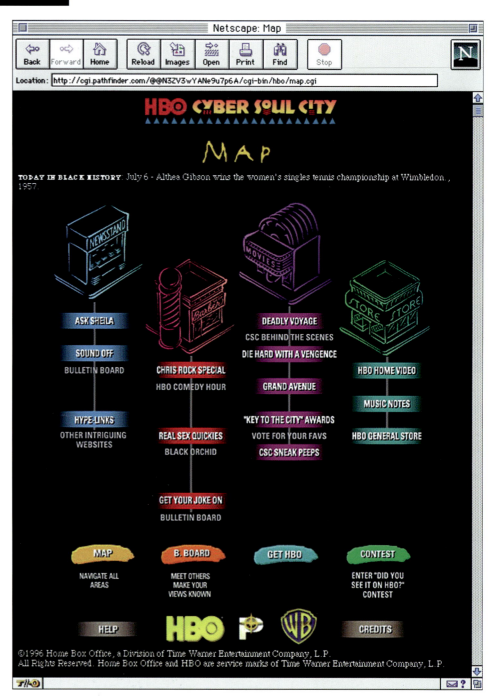

Icons that look like hand drawings are used for street corners and give access to each corner.

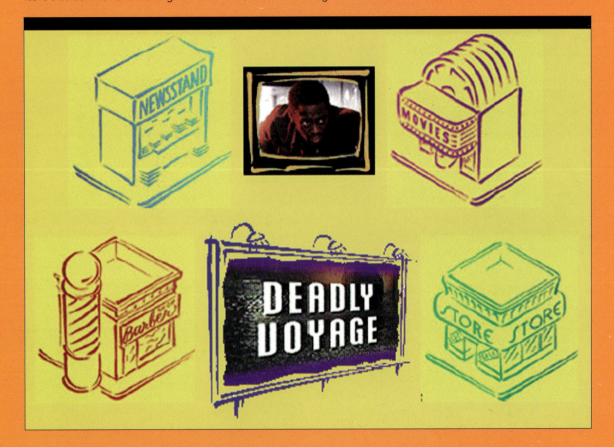

The making of a film titled DEADLY VOYAGE. (top)
After all, boxing is a popular sport among blacks. (top right)
HBO Strangers Contest, a quiz corner for viewers. (right)

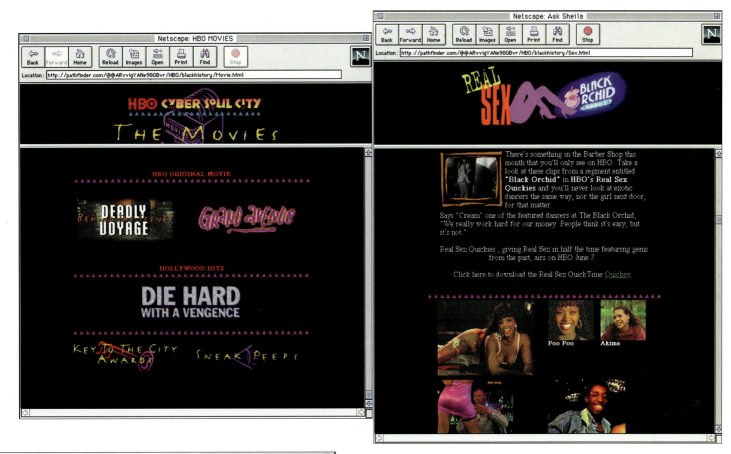

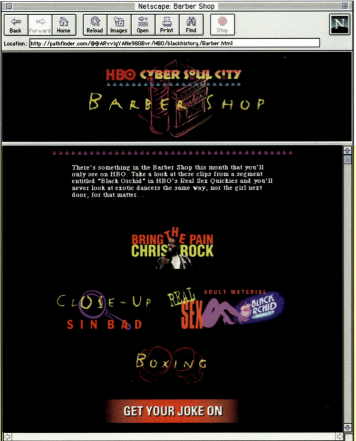

When you access THE MOVIES page, you see some film titles. (top left)
The most common topic in a BARBER SHOP is sports (bottom left), followed by entertainment. (top right)

www.aiga.com

AIGA Miami

(http://www.aiga.com/miami/default.html)
America Institute of Graphic Arts

This site was built up by AIGA (American Institute of Graphic Arts). I will focus on the homepages created by the Miami and New York branches.

AIGA Miami
Miami's homepage features colorful icons against a background of palm trees under the Southern sun. Many typographies are incorporated with various designs, yet the design is still a unified whole. Unfortunately, icons appear to be linked to the corners, but some of the pages have not yet been constructed. When they are complete, this site will certainly be worth seeing.

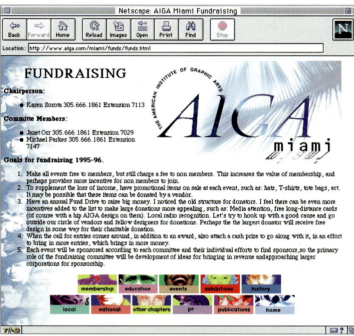

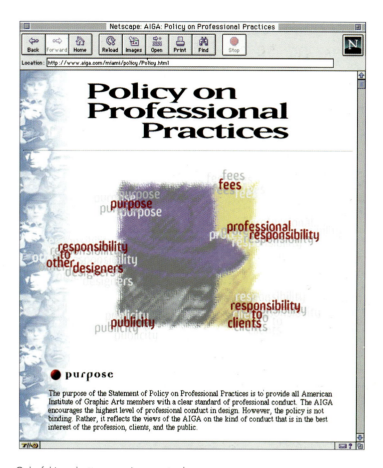

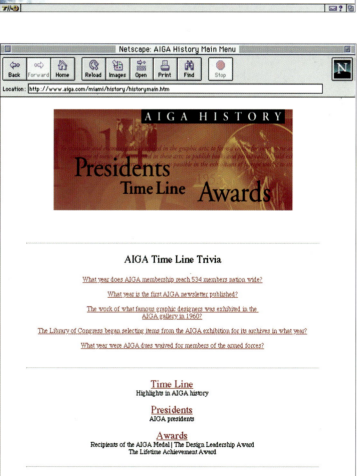

Colorful icon buttons serving as a tool map are arranged at the bottom of the page. (top left)
The Policy on Professional Practices page, in which long texts with many details are placed under this. (top right)

AIGA New York

(http://www.aiga.com/ny/default.html)
America Institute of Graphic Arts

Aiga New York's homepage is based on a layout using basic frames. The page was devised to make interfacing easy, and when you select something from the menu on the left, the information you want pops up within the framework on the right. The mostly monotone colors remind us of the speed and elegance of the big city of New York. This page, like that of the Miami branch, features a design built up with professional techniques.

This is the front page of the New York branch. A red NY is typed in a font that is different from the others and adds spice to the page. Although a royalty-free image was used, the designer's skill was great enough to make this page as appealing as it would have been had a less common image been used.

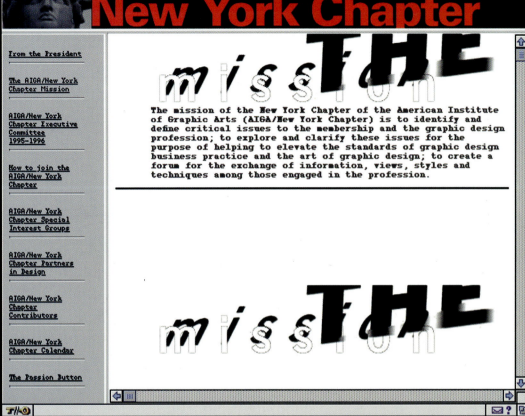

From the President

The AIGA/New York
Chapter Mission

AIGA/New York
Chapter Executive
Committee
1995-1996

How to join the
AIGA/New York
Chapter

AIGA/New York
Chapter Special
Interest Groups

AIGA/New York
Chapter Partners
in Design

AIGA/New York
Chapter
Contributors

AIGA/New York
Chapter Calendar

The Passion Button

The mission of the New York Chapter of the American Institute of Graphic Arts (AIGA/New York Chapter) is to identify and define critical issues to the membership and the graphic design profession; to explore and clarify these issues for the purpose of helping to elevate the standards of graphic design business practice and the art of graphic design; to create a forum for the exchange of information, views, styles and techniques among those engaged in the profession.

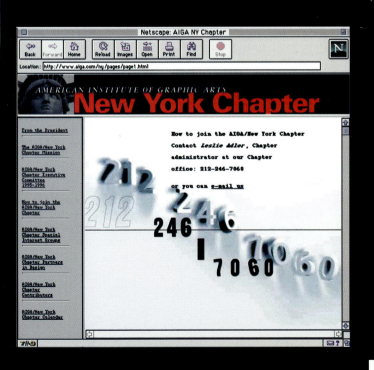

How to join the AIGA/New York Chapter
Contact *Leslie Adler*, Chapter administrator at our Chapter office: 212-246-7060

or you can e-mail us

The AIGA/NY Chapter *Passion Button* is public forum for the exchange of ideas, opinion and comment.

Questions and inquiries should be directed to the Chapt
212-246-7060.

www.ruse.com

RUSE Magazine

(http://www.ruse.com)

Design/Production Firm : the Code Syndicate
Art Director : Shawn C. Kim
Creative Director : Mallory EC Margueron
Copywriter : Shawn C. Kim
Designer : Shawn C. Kim / Mallory EC Margueron
Illustrator : Mallory EC Margueron
Photographer : J.D. Peterson
HTML Writer : Shawn C. Kim
Programmer : Shawn C. Kim

RUSE means tricks or scheme or deception, a strong-seeming title for the web site of a magazine dedicated to art and culture. At first, I couldn't understand it at all. But, pondering it with inquisitive eye, I finally got a feeling about it: the images in these pages hold hidden meanings; they are deeper, more mysterious than they appear to be. That is the RUSE.

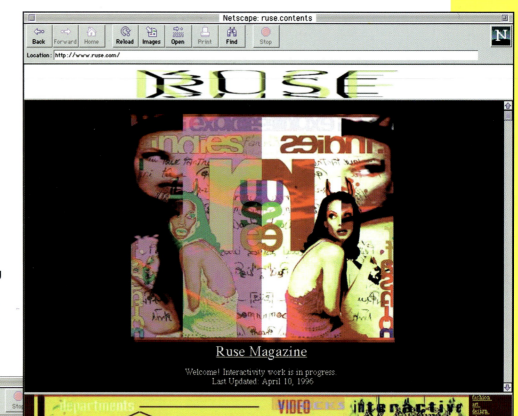

the Ocean's end | Two girls on a psychological exploration. summerwear
photos by JD* make-up by Terence* styling by Chelsea* models: malika & jennifer

cycle 181 | Folly in the washing room + dressed up at the club.
photos by Chris Brown* make-up by Raul* styling Don & Ruse* models: stephanie & natasha.

retro elegance | Studio layout featuring suits and corsets.
photos by Chris Brown* make-up by Raul* styling by Ruse & Khoi* models: ines, tracy & malika.

blur scapes | A photographic expedition of haute couture and landscapes.
photos by JD* make-up by Raul* styling by Don & Chelsea* models: tracy, berg & joy.

There are all kinds of web magazines, but RUSE is surely unique. It is elegant, and everything about it puts it in the vanguard of photogravure. The pages are full of big, beautiful images and contain a minimum of text, and every image is a complete work of art by itself. Thus, it is almost sure that, in these pages, there is something to be found that will appeal to everyone. It is true that downloading from RUSE can take some time, but what a small price to pay for such splendid art!

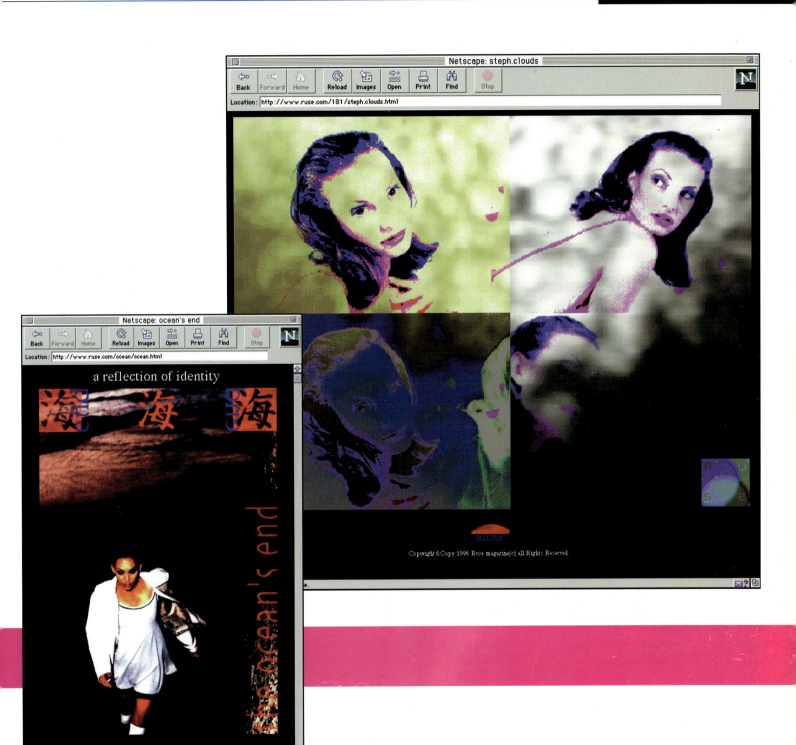

Netscape: ines.series

Location: http://www.ruse.com/brown/ines.html

San Francisco. Khoi Van Chow has done it all- from being Stevie Wonder's stylist to being David Hasselhoff's personal fashion coordinator to starting his own line of clothes under the label Kacyichi. Khoi's clothes are elegant in form and gives one the impression of Parisian nostalgia.

Wing Tip shoes from Gimme Shoes. Black Pin Striped suit by Khoi van Chow

Copyright© 1996 Ruse magazine(c) All Rights Reserved

Netscape: photo

Location: http://www.ruse.com/photo.html

ruse photo

the metro

exposure flash   streetsmoke

exposure flash | 3 portfolios of young photographers.

the Metro | A chilling series of digital artist MECM.

Streetsmoke | A daily photo-journal of urban style.

RUSE of ten uses transparent collages, and the multi-layered complexity of the images give shape to a unique world. These works of art, with their deep overlays of image and color, show a sophisticated taste and technique that is extraordinary.

Document : Done.

www.hi-d.com

HI-D

(http://www.hi-d.com)

Design/Production Firm : Hi-D
Client : Various and Hi-D
Art Director : Moki Cherry
Creative Director : Heidi Dangelmaier
Copywriter : Betty Oliver, and all above
Designer : Moki Cherry
Illustrator : Moki Cherry
HTML Writer :Heidi Dangelmaier
Programmer :
Heidi Dangelmaier,Timir Karia and Flow Research
Producer : Valerie Goodman

This page is full of strong impressive images. Each flat color illustration in a large format is placed with a text typed in a large font against a primary-color background. The page ignores preconceived ideas and never appears worried about the memory size of the graphic data. The images and text of the layout are well-balanced. I could feel the decisive attitude of the designers; it is as if they built up the page just as they liked. The screens of the browser are not a page, but a canvas for the designers. Their senses of color is so professional that no incongruity is ever felt. I am sure that this homepage will have a strong impact on viewers.

12/95 People magazine

Every illustration is dramatically large and powerful. Some of them are passionate and erotic.

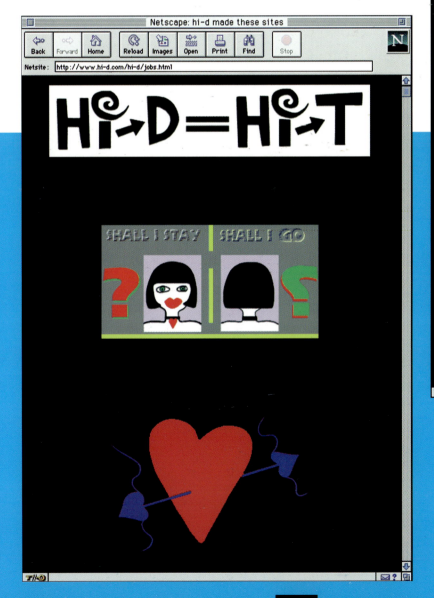

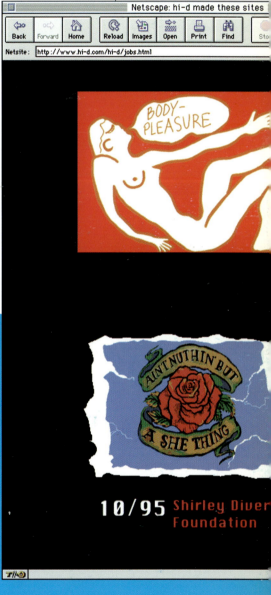

Both the title, Progressive Erotica. The design of a face and earrings portraying male and female symbols give off an extraordinary, somewhat difficult atmosphere. (right)

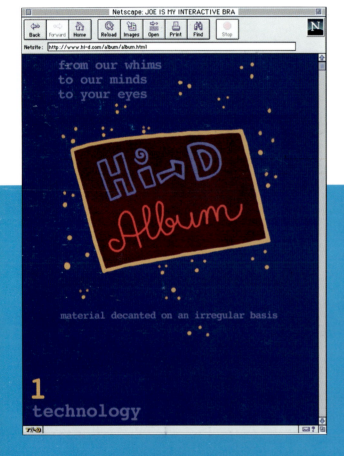

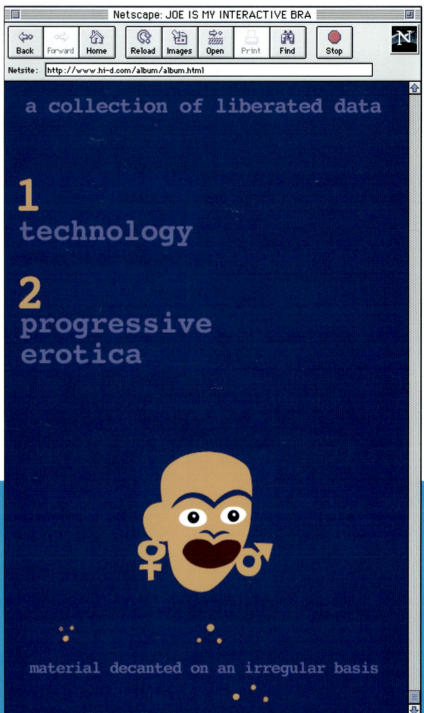

What is meaning of "JOE is my interactive bra" ?
How suggestive this title is ! (bottom left)

www.papermag.com

PAPERMAG
(http://www.papermag.com)

This is the online version of the New York-based town magazine, *Paper*. It shows a novel design with icons that make the most of the monitor's property. That is, transparent lights are used to create colors and images. Fluorescent color icons placed against a black background look like neon signs in the dark of night. Every image is so attractive and full of urban sensibility and the balance of image and text is so well done that the design is perfect and the result is a flawless whole. The wide range of topics covered include food, music, shop, club, cyber, and stage. If you plan to visit New York, it would be a very good idea to get information from this page before going.

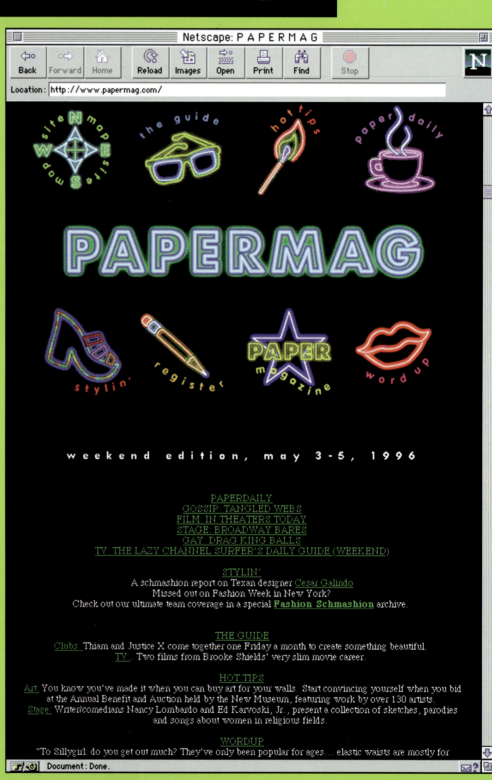

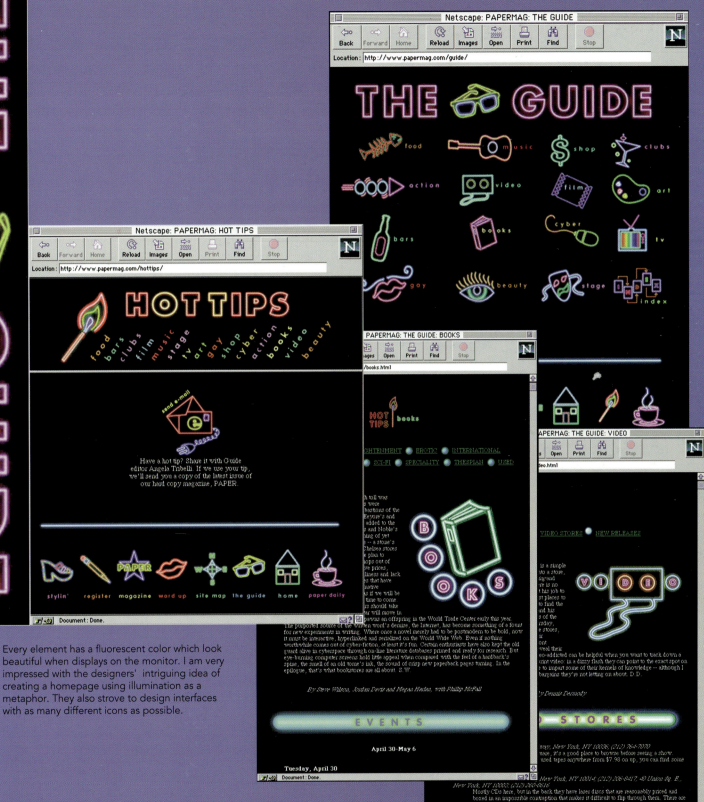

Every element has a fluorescent color which look beautiful when displays on the monitor. I am very impressed with the designers' intriguing idea of creating a homepage using illumination as a metaphor. They also strove to design interfaces with as many different icons as possible.

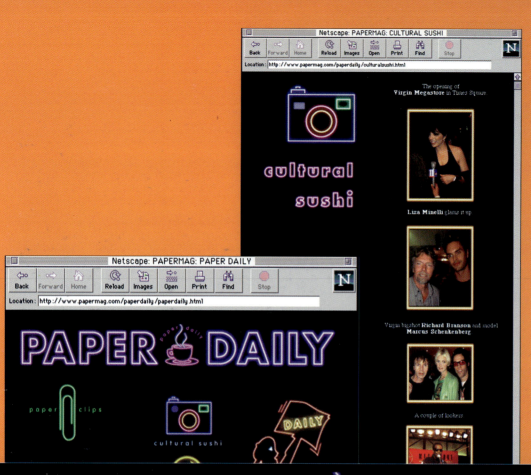

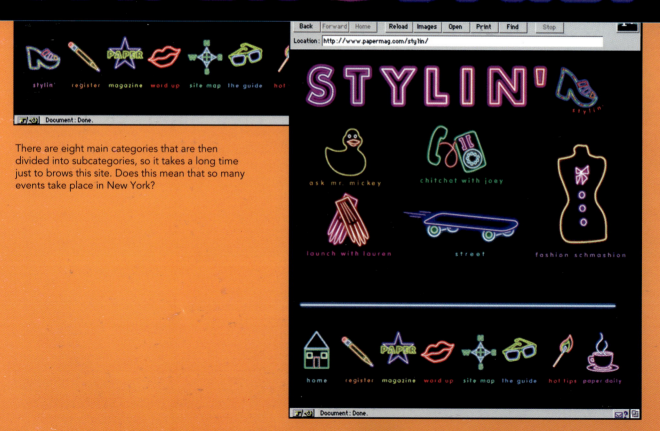

There are eight main categories that are then divided into subcategories, so it takes a long time just to brows this site. Does this mean that so many events take place in New York?

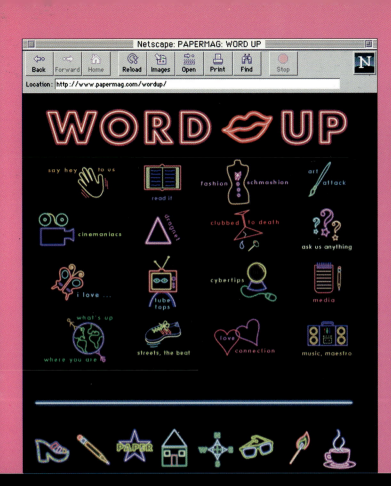

Netscape: PAPERMAG: WORD UP

Location: http://www.papermag.com/wordup/

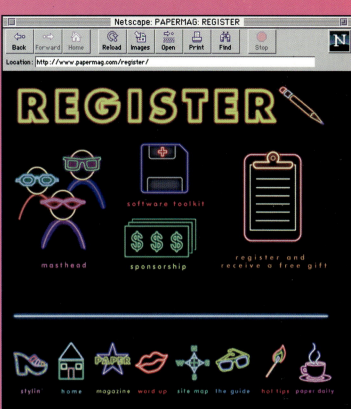

Netscape: PAPERMAG: REGISTER

Location: http://www.papermag.com/register/

WORD UP

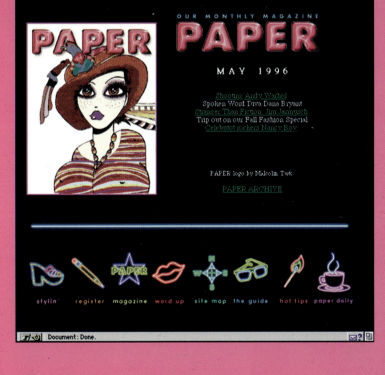

OUR MONTHLY MAGAZINE

PAPER

MAY 1996

Shooting Andy Warhol
Spoken Word Diva Dana Bryant
Stranger Than Fiction: Jim Jarmusch
Trip out on our Fall Fashion Special
Celebutot rockers Nancy Boy

PAPER logo by Malcolm Turk

PAPER ARCHIVE

Get a little taste of summer.   A|X ARMANI EXCHANGE

www.commarts.com

Communication Arts
The Essential Creative Resource

Communication Arts

(http://www.commarts.com)

This site is the online version of *Communication Arts*, one of the most popular design magazines in the United States. The homepage is linked to a vast amount of information about digital design. By referring to the database called Creative Resources, you can access the homepages which were created by famous designers and well-known production companies. The icon buttons with rectangular color blocks and a simple practical layout create a clean feeling. This homepage has much to teach designers.

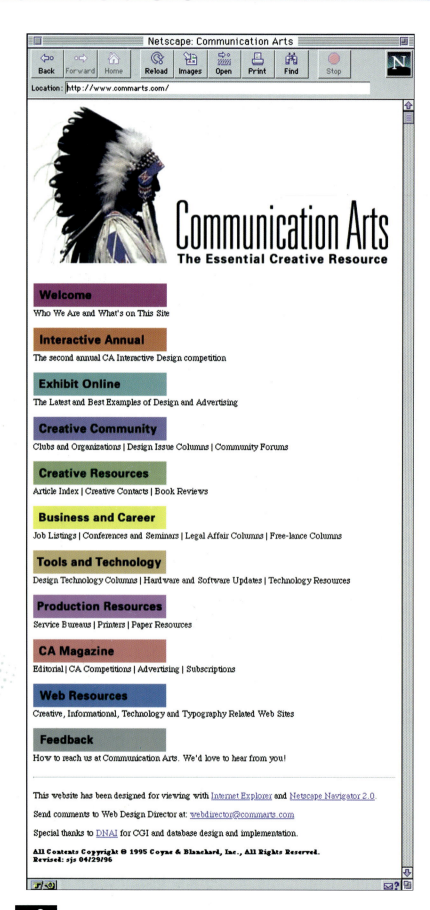

Welcome

Who We Are and What's on This Site

Welcome to the World Wide Web site for *Communication Arts*, the world's largest magazine on creativity for graphic designers, art directors, copywriters, photographers, illustrators and multimedia designers. This site is much more than just a reuse of existing content from the magazine, it's an extensive online resource for creative professionals to enhance their work and careers and a catalyst for bringing community to visual communicators around the world.

For those new to our site, the following is a brief description of the content you can find here:

Exhibit Online
A showcase of the latest and best examples of design and advertising. In addition to background information and full creative credits, you can click on thumbnails to view full-screen images of the featured projects.

Creative Community
You can search a national database of clubs and organizations to connect with people in your area.

Read a series of thought-provoking "Design Issue" columns discussing topics relevant to the field of visual communications.

Use our Community Forums to view and respond to ideas, problems and solutions faced by other members of the creative community.

Creative Resources
Search for inspiration and information with a database of articles, columns and Exhibit projects that have appeared in *Communication Arts* magazine in the last ten years.

Use our Creative Contacts database to find design firms, advertising agencies, photographers, illustrators and multimedia developers whose work has [...] last two years.

To help you in researching a particular subject, use our [...] technology that we've reviewed in *Communication A[...]*

Business and Career
We've included a list of positions available as well as s[...]

To enhance your business and career and expand your [...] of upcoming conferences and events.

We've posted articles from Tad Crawford, our legal af[...] information on legal issues pertaining to visual commu[...]

Exhibit Online

United States Postal Service commemorative stamp in honor of women's suffrage and the passage of the amendment. "When the Citizen's Stamp Advisory Committee (CSAC) recommended the subject of Women's Suffrage be included in our 1995 commemorative stamp program, the next step was to refer the project to the D[...] Subcommittee to determine the feasibility of visualizing the subject in the size of a stamp," stated Elizabeth A. Altobell, United States Postal Service representative. "That committee includes leaders in the field of design. M[...] the proponents for the stamp wanted something innovative and abstract and April Greiman's name was propose[...] artist to be considered."

Carl Herrman, art director; April Greiman, designer/writer/creative director; various photographers; Greimanski Labs, Los Angeles, design firm.

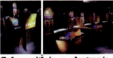

[Click to view three larger images. 14k, 21k & 23k]

Cybersmith is an electronic environment where consumers can experience the latest computer technolog[...] Customers can experiment with the Internet, online services, cd-rom titles, games and more. The On Line Cafe features drinks, snacks and light meals that can be ordered from the computer stations. "As part of development activities for their second store location, Cybersmith was seeking two creative resources: one to develop the use[...] interface for in-store experiences and online travel, and a second to develop an in-store graphic communication system," said Shirley Rogers, spokesperson for Fitch, Inc. "Cybersmith approached Fitch with regard to the interactive work and was surprised to find that teams within the same Fitch office were doing work in both new[...] communication systems. The repositioning of the store included a be[...] just a destination but an activity. The positioning led to a tagline --

[...]g/Betty Lin/Jean-Andre Villamizar, designers; Mike [...] Meade, creative directors; Mark Steele photographer; [...] [...]vartz Silver, architect.

[...]es. 43k, 55k]

a biweekly Internet magazine of books, art and ideas. The [...]

Interactive Annual

inter*active* design annual **2**

The colorful icons on the left side of the page are placed vertically. Each color block is linked to header image on each related page. Though the design is very simple, the color blocks work effectively adding accent to the page. (opposite)

www.hypermode.com

Hypermode

(http://www.hypermode.com)

Editor : Tom Kincaid
Fashion Editors : Nicole Lombardo, Sarah Parlow
Beauty Editor : Meli Pennington
Head Writer : James Krieg
Photographers : Akira Miyauchi, Yvonne Lo
Make-up Artists : Yukie Hashimoto, Tamami Mihara
Graphic Artist : Ernie Parada

Usually a site in the fashion line is built up from a paper layout, but Hypermode has made full use of the frame function of computers. Its icon buttons set against a metallic color background have a real computer look, as if the page is trying to create a medium beyond print. It can be argued either way as to whether the experiment is successful, but in any case, as this homepage makes use of many high-quality fashion photogravures, we are sure to enjoy it.

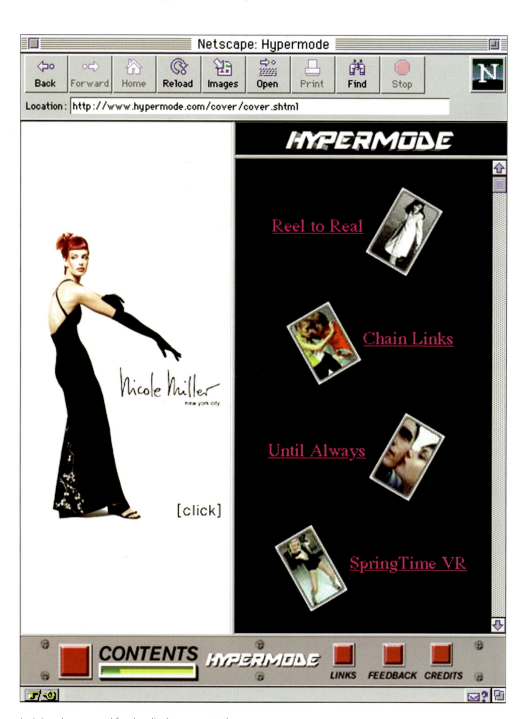

Isn't it rather unusual for the display screen to be divided vertically into two parts? To me, the beautiful woman and solid color buttons at the bottom of the screen fail to harmonize.

Netscape: Hypermode/Reel to Real

Back | Forward | Home | Reload | Images | Open | Print | Find | Stop

Location: http://www.hypermode.com/movie/movie_start.html

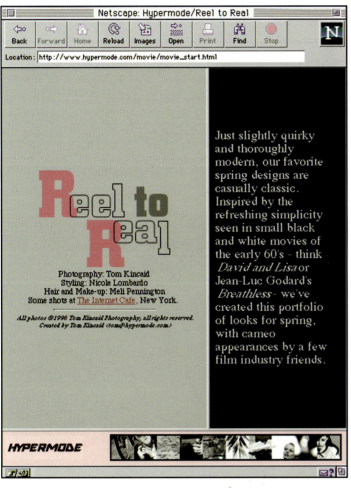

Reel to Real

Photography: Tom Kincaid
Styling: Nicole Lombardo
Hair and Make-up: Meli Pennington
Some shots at The Internet Cafe, New York.

*All photos ©1996 Tom Kincaid Photography, all rights reserved.
Created by Tom Kincaid <tom@hypermode.com>*

Just slightly quirky and thoroughly modern, our favorite spring designs are casually classic. Inspired by the refreshing simplicity seen in small black and white movies of the early 60's - think *David and Lisa* or Jean-Luc Godard's *Breathless* - we've created this portfolio of looks for spring, with cameo appearances by a few film industry friends.

HYPERMODE

Netscape: Hypermode/Until Always

Back | Forward | Home | Reload | Images | Open | Print | Find | Stop

Location: http://www.hypermode.com/cgi-bin/always.pl

until always

Photography: Georgia Kokolis
Styling: Barbara Eisen
Make-up: Meli Pennington
Hair: Laurie Hefner

Janelle/Ford wears a pink linen duster and pink linen drawstring skirt from Gabriella Zanzani collection. Joseph/Ford wears a blanket from Ikea.

HYPERMODE

http://www.hypermode.com/hm1_2/stvr.html

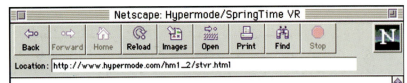

SpringTime VR

Featuring the Spring collection from Times 7 by Todd Oldham with cruise wear by Norma Kamali and Robespiere and shoes by Kenneth Cole and Susan, Bennis, Warren, Edwards.

SpringTime VR

Photography and computer stuff: Tom Kincaid
Styling: Nicole Lombardo
Hair and Make-up: Tamami Mihara
Model: Susan Nicholson/Company
Studio: GO Rental Studio, New York, 212-564-4084

QuickTime VR is an exciting new technology from Apple that allows you to experience three-dimensional scenes and it's as easy as...

 1 If you haven't already, download the free player software (available for Mac or Windoze) from Apple's QuickTime VR site.

 2 Now download the high resolution (710K) or low resolution (88K) version of the SpringTime VR scene.

 3 Have a look around. Use your mouse or arrow keys to turn, option to zoom in and control to zoom out.

HYPERMODE

Document: Done.

---

http://www.hypermode.com/hm1_2/adv_start.html

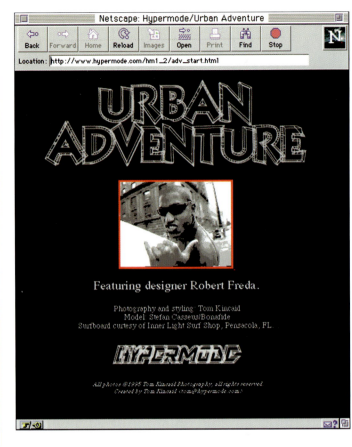

URBAN ADVENTURE

Featuring designer Robert Freda.

Photography and styling: Tom Kincaid
Model: Stefan Casseus/Bonafide
Surfboard curtesy of Inner Light Surf Shop, Pensacola, FL.

HYPERMODE

---

http://www.hypermode.com/hm1_1/hm1cg12.html

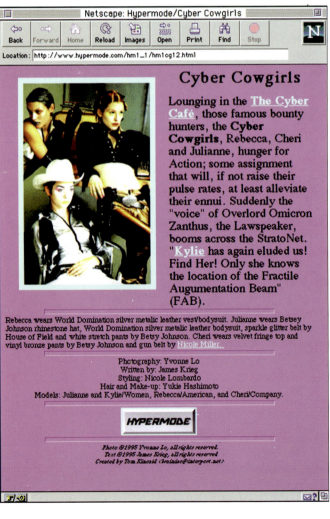

Cyber Cowgirls

Lounging in the The Cyber Café, those famous bounty hunters, the **Cyber Cowgirls**, Rebecca, Cheri and Julianne, hunger for Action; some assignment that will, if not raise their pulse rates, at least alleviate their ennui. Suddenly the "voice" of Overlord Omicron Zanthus, the Lawspeaker, booms across the StratoNet. "Kylie has again eluded us! Find Her! Only she knows the location of the Fractile Augmentation Beam" (FAB).

Rebecca wears World Domination silver metalic leather vest/bodysuit. Julianne wears Betsey Johnson rhinestone hat, World Domination silver metalic leather bodysuit, sparkle glitter belt by House of Field and white stretch pants by Betsy Johnson. Cheri wears velvet fringe top and vinyl bronze pants by Betsy Johnson and gun belt by Nicole Miller.

Photography: Yvonne Lo
Written by: James Krieg
Styling: Nicole Lombardo
Hair and Make-up: Yukie Hashimoto
Models: Julianne and Kylie/Women, Rebecca/American, and Cheri/Company.

HYPERMODE

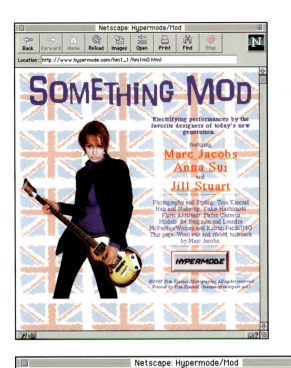

SOMETHING MOD

Electrifying performances by the favorite designers of today's new generation.

featuring

Marc Jacobs
Anna Sui
and
Jill Stuart

Photography and Styling: Tom Kincaid
Hair and Make-up: Yukie Hashimoto
Photo Assistant: Stefan Casseus
Models: Be Bergman and Leandra
McPartlan/Women and Kristin Pazik/IMG
This page: Wool suit and ribbed turtleneck
by Marc Jacobs.

HYPERMODE

The essence of
MOD
transmuted from
London's East End
in the *early* 60's
to the
catwalks
of the
90's.

Essential music:
The **Who**
and
the Kinks
Essential accessory:
a **Vespa**.

This is the homepage for introducing model images recorded by QuickTime VR technology. The photographers took the picture by placing the camera in the middle of the room and the models around the camera. It is no exaggeration to say that a novel idea like this demonstrates the power of the latest technologies to their fullest advantage.

www.stim.com

stim

(http://www.stim.com)

This homepage managed by Prodigy, a PC communication enterprise, is a new online magazine targeted at young people. A lot of cheerful icons and photographs are used in every corner: Static, which is full of articles composed mainly of text; a bulletin board and chat corner; a video conference room, CU SeeMe; a DYNAMIC corner, full of devices that only the Internet can make. This page should be very attractive to the younger generation in the U.S., but it seems almost too cheerful and makes me dizzy. It seems that Prodigy is trying too hard to be in touch with the Internet age and culture in their attempt to capture the hearts of young people. Still, despite that criticism, the site is rich with wonderfully elaborated contents. When Japanese youngsters start making serious online magazines sponsored by major companies, the present situation will be improved, and I look forward to more exciting presentations.

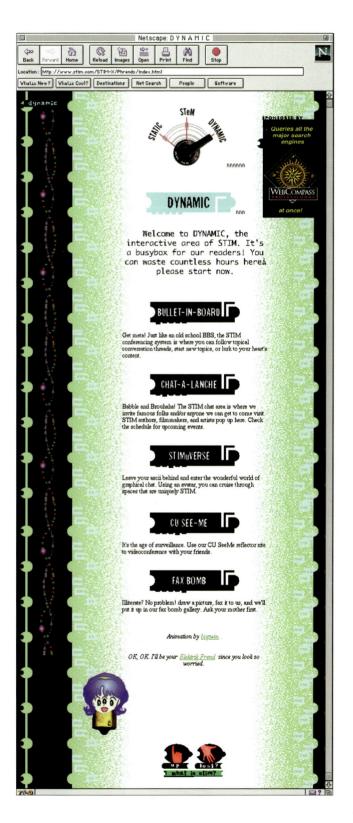

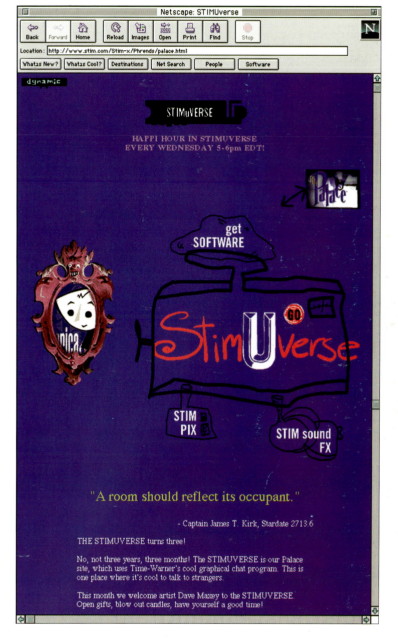

Interestingly, you can see at the bottom left of the screen an illustration similar to Japanese animation. (left)
The Table of Contents is composed completely of images. It seems easy to identify the corners have somewhat tricky English names. (left on opposite page)

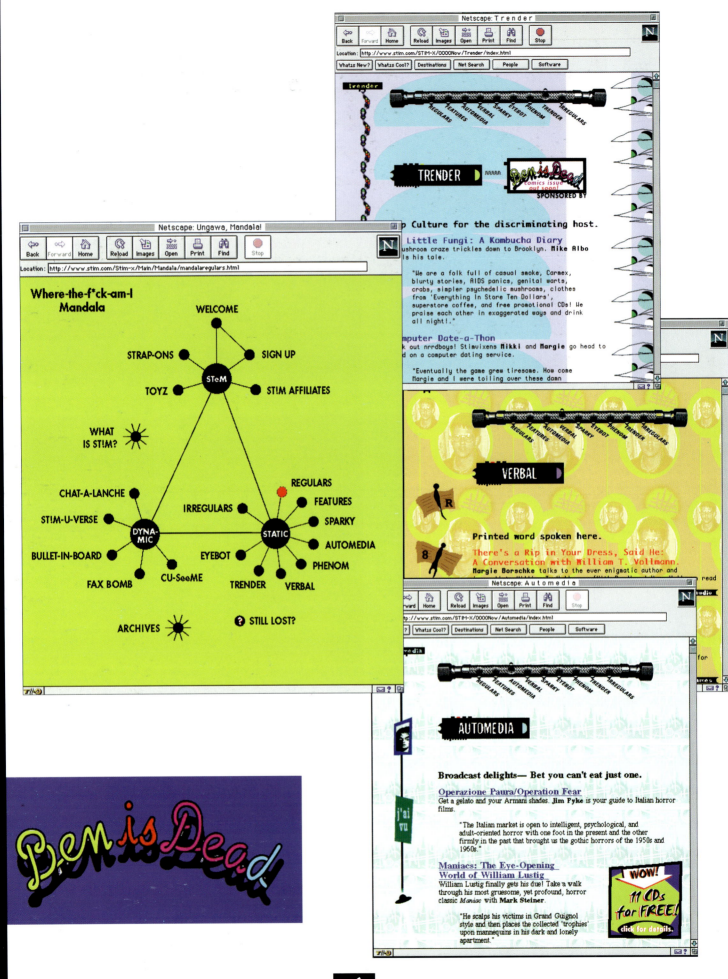

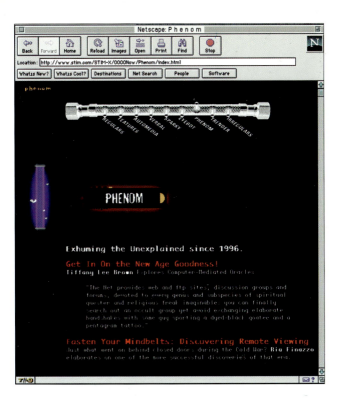

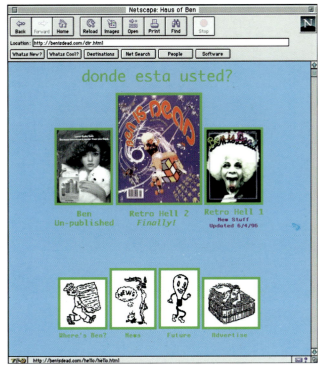

The contents look like food that we can eat. Every image has a super loud cartoon-like design. The background is filled with various patterns. It is, indeed, American pop culture. I am impressed by the variety and extent of the contents, but most of the topics seems rather insignificant.

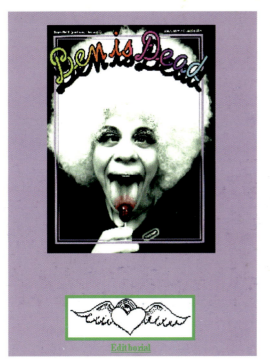

www.lumiere.com

Lumière

Lumiere

(http://www.lumiere.com)

Design/Production Firm : Triple International Inc.
Client : Triple International Inc.
(Lumiere is a publication of Triple International.)
Creative Director : Thomas Lenthal
Writers :
Stephen Todd, Ian Phillips, Lee Tulloch, among others.
Photographers :
Jean-Baptiste Mondino, Nick Knight, Paolo Roversi,
Enrique Badulesco, among others.
HTML and programming : Triple International Inc.

This is the online version of a fashion magazine that features the highest quality photogravures and articles well worth reading. The site consists of FASHION, BEAUTY and ARTS corners, and you can see beautiful pictures and texts against a black background on every page. The articles cover many well-known fashion designers, including Galliano and Jil Sander. Judging from totality of this site, I believe that over 50% of the users are women. Not limited to this site, homepages related to fashion in general are very skillful in the selection and layout of photogravures and illustrations as well as the overall presentation. It may be that the site is so lovely because the fashion business seeks to create beauty. However, considering that were able to display their full power, even in this new-born media which is so different from other traditional ones, I must admire their eye for beauty.

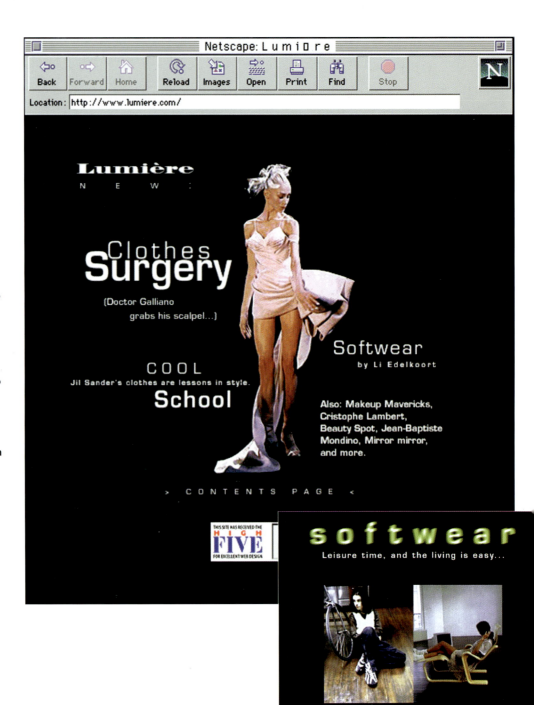

Lumière
FASHION

Sharp Cuts, Not Short Cuts
Paris Men's Ready-to-Wear collections

Clothes Surgery
(Doctor Galliano grabs his scalpel...)

Softwear
With the softening of lines between employment and leisure comes a need for new clothing and interiors... explains Li Edelkoort.

Cool School
Jil Sander's minimal clothes are lessons in modern elegance.

Mondino: Freeze-frame on fashion's future.
What do Madonna, Björk and Neneh Cherry have in common? Jean-Baptiste Mondino!

Mirror, mirror...
Lumière's readers ask how to be the fairest of them all

To see Lumière's earlier articles, click here.

FEEDBACK

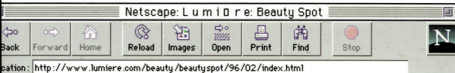

Netscape: L u m i ô r e : Beauty Spot

Back | Forward | Home | Reload | Images | Open | Print | Find | Stop

Location: http://www.lumiere.com/beauty/beautyspot/96/02/index.html

beauty SPOT

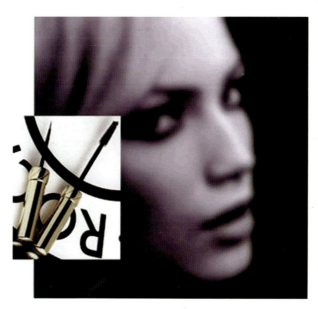

Black
'aint black

Inspired by the mysterious beauties
Rochas have come up with a new line
matching mascaras. At first sight al
innocently black. But after some inv
'mystery of the faux noirs' it turns
not always, well...black.

Instead, there is **Noir Violi**
enriched with a pigment cockta
and vivid violet that gives br
'je ne sais quoi'. **Noir Fumé,**
shimmer of gold and bronze, is
for deadly blondes. And then t
black black **Noir Extrême** wit
mother of pearl for the girls
compromise. With the new shade

Document: Done.

North Star Rising
Christophe Lambert talks to Lumière about fast food, French film and ...fun.

By Ian Phillips

www.dag.nl/dutch

DUTCH ON-LINE

(http://www.dag.nl/dutch)
Design/Production Firm :Datageneration
Client : Art View
Art Director : Peter vd Hoogen, Wim Bertram
Designer :Peter vd Hoogen, Wim Bertram
HTML Writer :Peter vd Hoogen, Wim Bertram
Programmer : Vincent Hillenbrink

This is the online version of a fashion and lifestyle magazine from the Netherlands. The homepage features a beautiful layout and neat design, in which photographic images with a refined sense of taste are processed and pleasantly placed. This homepage is located in the same site as 1000% Max or Data Generation. (http://www.dag.nl/)

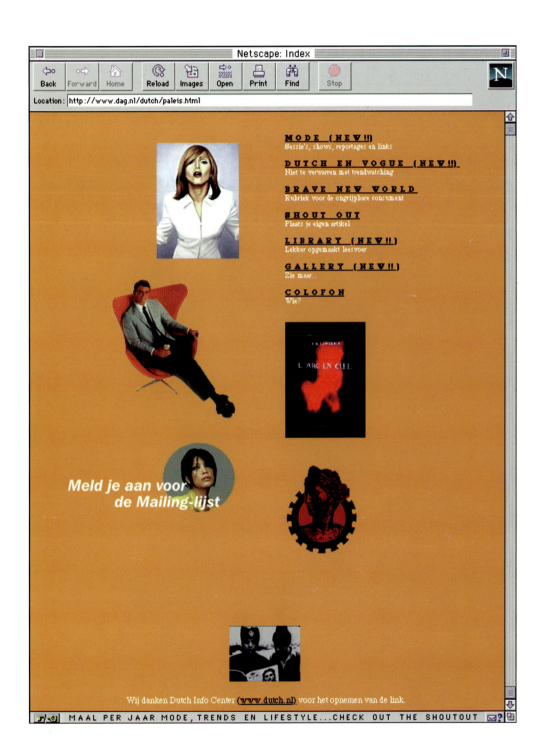

D u † c H

Netscape: Mode

Back Forward Home Reload Images Open Print Find Stop

Location: http://www.dag.nl/dutch/mode.html

MODE

Spring fashion 96:Anything goes!

Cocktales

Two pictures from:

Hunt

Chelsea Lads

Flashback

Guestpages:

Orson &bodil

Index

Document: Done.

Since the articles are written in Dutch, I cannot understand them, but images appealing to fashion-sensitive people are universally understood even without words. This also seems like a proof tat globalization is progressing.

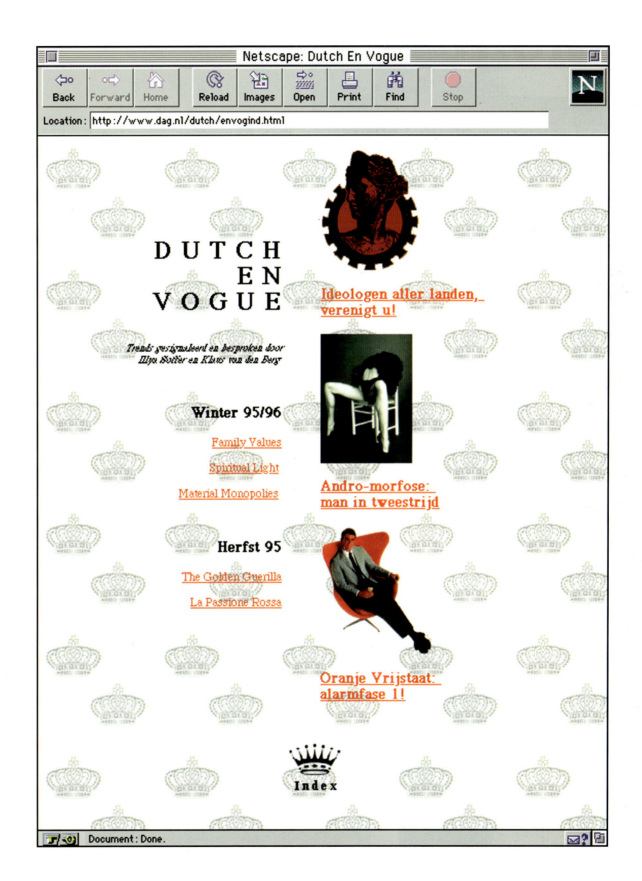

WWV
fash

fashion.uk

(http://www.widemedia.co

Design/Production Firm : Ikon
Client : self-published
Art Director : Owen Valentine F
Creative Director : Brad Sidey
Copywriter : Marian Buckley, V
Designer : Ben Edwards
Photographer : Verity McIlveen
HTML Writer :
Ben Edwards, Brad Sidey, Owe
Programmer : Ben Edwards
Others : Emilie Selbourne, Sloa

**Most online magazine:
fashion-industry sites
because they are full of
pictures, and this is ce
with Fashion UK. Man:
fresh images are used
(fashion shoots, hot sh
health and beauty, fea
links page, you can se
other fashion-industry**

This features three famous male designers in the
U. K. The fashion shown here is conventional
enough that everyone can wear it. The words "All
are refreshingly 'unfash' and low key" might be
added. (top, middle, bottom)

A shot showing the t
fashion.

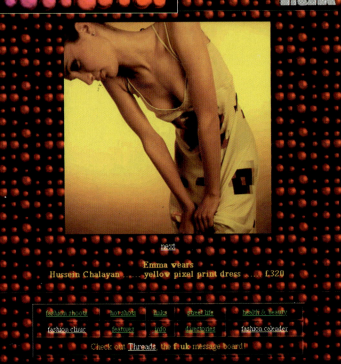

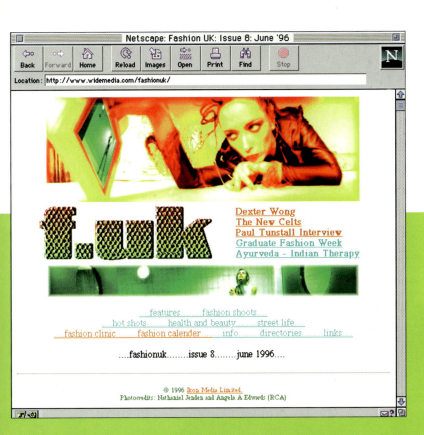

f.uk

Dexter Wong
The New Celts
Paul Tunstall Interview
Graduate Fashion Week
Ayurveda - Indian Therapy

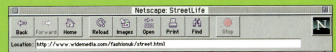

...features....... fashion shoots....
...hot shots....... health and beauty....... street life....
fashion clinic....... fashion calender..... info..... directories....... links....

....fashionuk........issue 8........june 1996....

© 1996 Ikon Media Limited.
Photocredits: Nathaniel Jenden and Angela A Edwards (RCA)

The new breed of Celtic designers work with non-traditional fabrics and don't sell their wares as souvenirs. Celtic is an Indo-European family of languages which includes Gaelic and Welsh and Breton and the Celtic tradition dates back to pre-Roman times when speakers of Celtic languages inhabited Britain, Gaul, Spain and other parts of Western Europe. Although there are only a few places left where these languages are still spoken, a strong affection for Celtic art, icons and mythology remains.

Celtic Rebel

Kathleen Readman's work re-interprets her Celtic roots. Brought up in Yorkshire she moved to her mother's homeland, Scotland, to study design. "I get so sick of seeing all this Scottish stuff," she says. "You only have to stroll down the Royal Mile and it's in your face. People assume because you are studying in Edinburgh you're bound to make everything tartan-looking."

Despite eschewing traditional Scottish design, Kathleen does feel that working in Edinburgh is crucial for inspiration. "Edinburgh gives me space. Here you're not pushed in any one direction and you're free from the pressures of London." Kathleen's Final collection is based on an story she found on the Internet entitled 'Angels Amongst Us'. The mythology of guardian angels is explored in a cream pieces while yellow and black pieces evoke evil angels. "I wanted to create a winged effect," she explains, "so I used 300 silk flowers which I bought in Levis', took them apart and then layered them. It took me ages to do."

Kathleen's earlier work concentrated on alternative wedding wear - "which looks more like club wear" and while she claims her collections "steer clear of Celtic origins" feels her background facilities her ideas. "The diversity means you have a lot to offer - but these days marketing has become so important."

● For more information call Kathleen on 0131 221 6131.

Catherine Bond - Irish Style

Knitwear designer Catherine Bond was born and bred in Belfast. Specialising in unconventional hats, jumpers and scarves, she claims "the Celtic influence is there in my work but I try not to make too much of it. There are a lot of aran sweaters around and I try to steer clear from that sort of thing!" As well as Irish yarns, Catherine uses Irish linen. "My 'pocket sweater' is made from linen with upside down pockets and real pockets all over it. I do follow Celtic tradition in the way I make good quality natural-looking clothes. The Irish are known for quality work and I try to live up to that."

Catherine's commitment to quality workmanship has influenced her design techniques. "I feel because I'm knitting a fabric first then making it into a wearable piece, I try to do something that no one else has done. I try to take something that makes people stop and ask 'Is that really knitted?'. I experiment a lot." Taking traditional skills and fabrics and modernising the process Catherine achieves a contemporary look. "You'll never find me doing cables," she promises and refuses to be lured by the leprechauns of nostalgia.

"I did some work at the Kilkenny Mills and it was so geared towards traditional Irish knits I felt it was really granny. To be honest people

---

f.uk

Tokyo Trippers

NICOLE MANASSEH spots the fashion conscious cruising in downtown Tokyo.

The Coca Cola Kids

Two 17 year old hat fans neck plenty of their favourite soft drink and finish off their outfits with just the right carrier bag. Check out those pouts!

The Casual Crew

Three 18 year old friends are out bargain-hunting. Heralding the return of flip flops and phat dungarees with matching large socks, it's a sporty but casual look.

Soul Bros

Ohashi (right) is 21 years old and loves Hip Hop and Rasta fashion. His impressive dreds cost 35,000 yen (about £300). His homie in the cool shirt wanted to remain anonymous.

This is the cover of the eighth issue published in June 1996. The thematic colors vary with every issue, here being lime green, yellow, and white. (top left)
Tokyo Trippers is the feature story on young fashion in Tokyo.

www.supermodel.com

SUPERMODEL.COM

SUPERMODEL.COM

(http://www.supermodel.com)

The word "supermodel" has become more familiar in Japan than ever before here. There have long been many sites covering the latest news and photographs of supermodels on to Internet and WWW. Is this any wonder considering that most users accessing from computer terminals at school are young male students or researchers? From such sites, we can get data about Cindy, Naomi Campbell, Claudia Schiffer, etc. It is surely bold for the producers to have named the site Supermodel, but the total design is as beautiful as a gorgeous fashion photogravure magazine. Before making any comments on the layouts or icons, etc., I want to say that male users probably feel happy to look at pictures of the most beautiful women of the century wearing swimsuits and popping up on the screen one after the another. This homepage is elaborately constructed, and you can see various types of pages, from a somewhat personal page featuring one of the models (Monika Schnarre) to a page called Supermodels in the Rainforest. This was shot on location in a tropical rainforest, and from it, we can get a good idea about the difficulty of shooting on location. This inside story is rather moving and most enjoyable to watch. Additionally, there is a News Wire page, featuring the latest trends and activities of top models and an Online Shops page, where you can buy various kinds of goods.

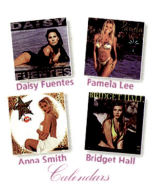

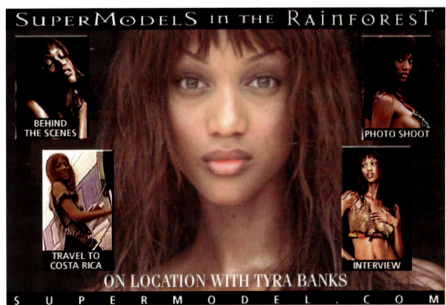

This is the personal page featuring Monika Schnarre. Looking at this beautiful woman, there can't be any complaints.

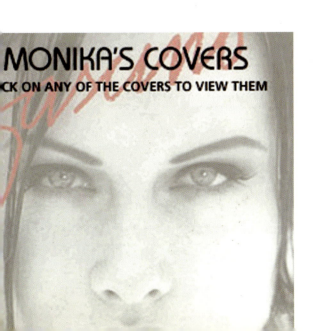

www.word.com

WORD

(http://www.word.com)

Design/Production Firm : ICon CMT Corp.

Word is as popular a site as Hot Wired among the online magazines focusing on young culture. The site is so popular that many leading companies, such as Microsoft and BMW, sponsor its ads. Apparently, the site can afford to keep uploading a vast amount of new information, and it always tries to please its users. Its most outstanding feature is its spirit of anticipation. Though ordinary menu icons are aligned vertically on the left side of the page, we can always discover elaborate devices somewhere in the site if we look closely. For example, we can move icons by using Server Push or Animation GIF or add HTML tag to the layout.

The site has no consistent pattern of design, but a suitable visual expression to each article may be observed, nevertheless. There are many familiar grungy-looking visuals from the 1990s, and each article has a strong impact. The contents cover a variety of topics. This site, provided by New York, is a must for anyone interested in the youth culture.

In this layout, the HTML tag is set up in many places. The circular illustrations aligned vertically on the left side of the page are shortcut icon buttons linked to each corner. The 3-D yellow icon image wit a smiling face (top middle of the page) repeats various humorous movements.

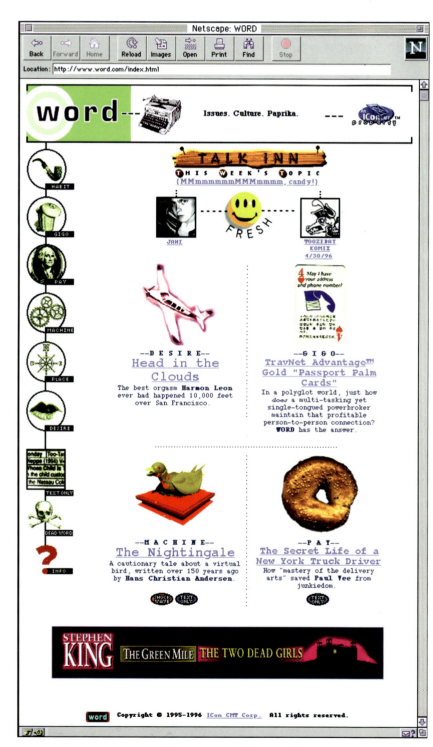

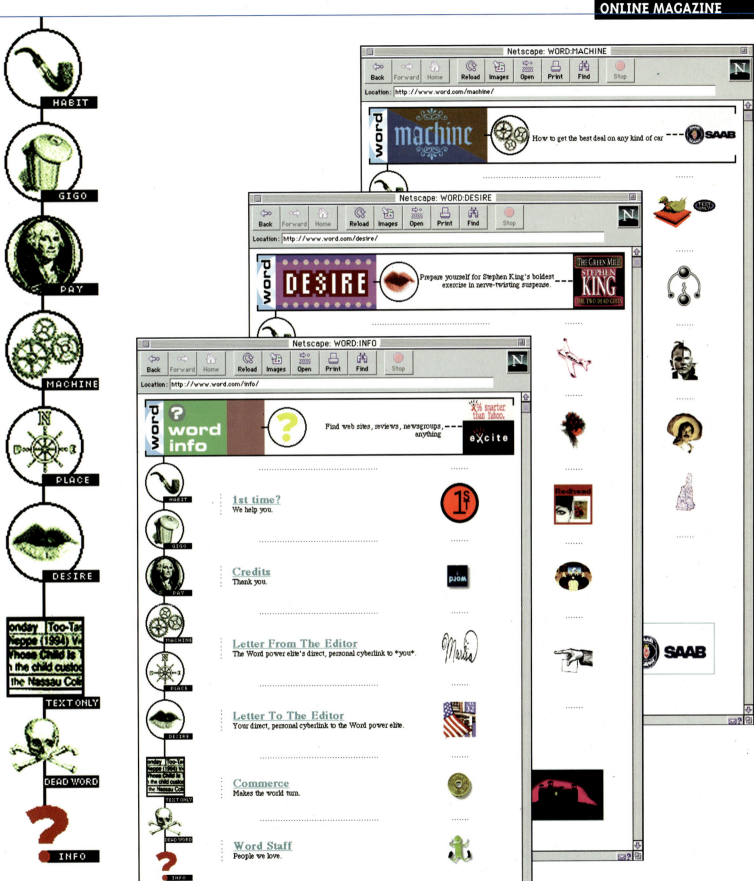

www.youmag.com

You Amok

(http://www.youmag.com)

"Warning: Do no attempt any of the body modifications or sexual practices described herein. If you feel compelled to attempt any of the hazardous practices described herein, please contact a professional therapist for treatment. Neither the contributors, editor, or publisher assumes responsibility for the use or misuse of any information in this magazine."
The homepage of You Magazine begins with the warning above. Its dramatic design, which combines ultra-powerful images and large fonts, is full of energy, although, with titles such as Sudden Death Masturbation, Amputees and Devotees, and Xenolingual Autoeroticism, the atmosphere is highly suspicious. The homepage closely reflects the youth culture of the 90s.

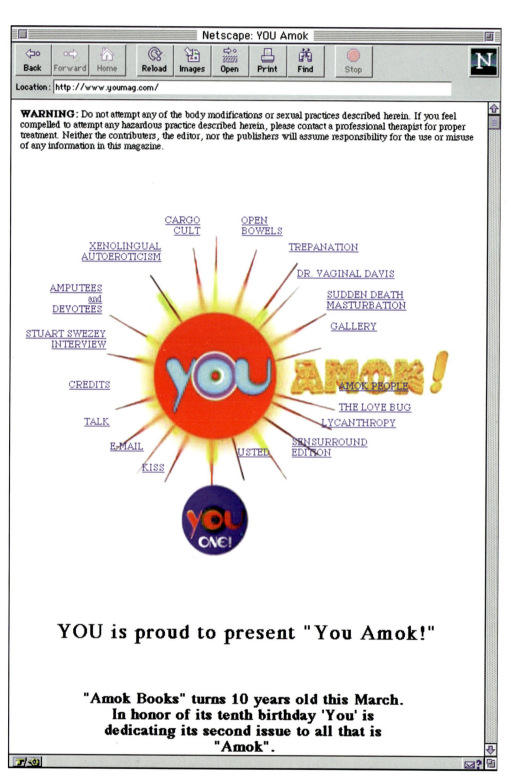

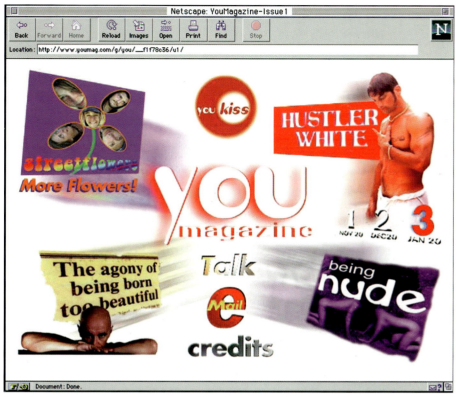

Although we may feel that its layout is too dramatic and sometimes rough, we never feel that it is shabby because every image used is of high quality. On the People page, the highlight is the layout, with a vast amount of photographic data aligned. If the speed of your computer is high enough, recommend that you access this site.

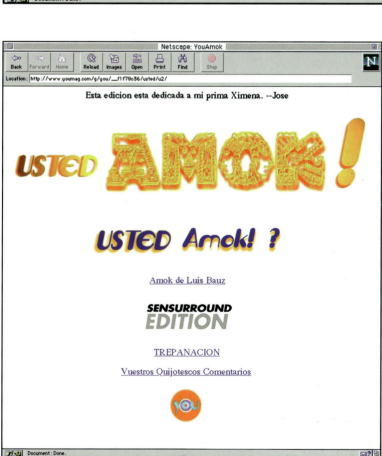

Gallery

W.P. Davis

peter novak

Ann Elliott Cutting

The exhibited work shall not be copied or reproduced without permission of the artist

This is a system of digital postcards with 25 images from which viewers select the one they like, add their message, and mail it. If you select from the middle along the top row, you can get the darling face of a young boy. (top right on opposite page)

Netscape: YouAmok - People

Back Forward Home Reload Images Open Print Find Stop

Location: http://www.youmag.com/g/you/__3205f38o/u2/features/ap/

stuart

melissa

you kiss

luis

you

The Sensurround Edition
by Kyle Roderick

Every era is embodied by its great, brain-boggling books. Before World War II, culture vultures, scholars, kids and kooks surfed the 1910 - 1911 Encyclopedia Britannica for info thrills, esoteric chills and multi-culti vibrations. As our shape-shifting planetary culture morphs into the 21st century, today's analogue to the Britannica is the recently published AMOK Journal: Sensurround Edition.

"Experienced" in the mind-fuckingly festive Jimi Hendrixian sense of the word, The Journal embodies the heart, mind and soul of our life and time: the Second Millenium. Sacred and profane information extremes, ideological dossiers and psycho-physiological investigations-- they all resonate here in stranger-than-true splendor. Cruising through this diverse freeway of souls and their ideas, one hears the ghost of the great modernist writer and voluptuary Oscar Wilde murmuring, "Nothing human is foreign to me."

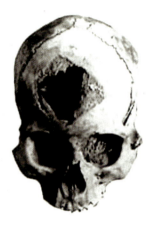

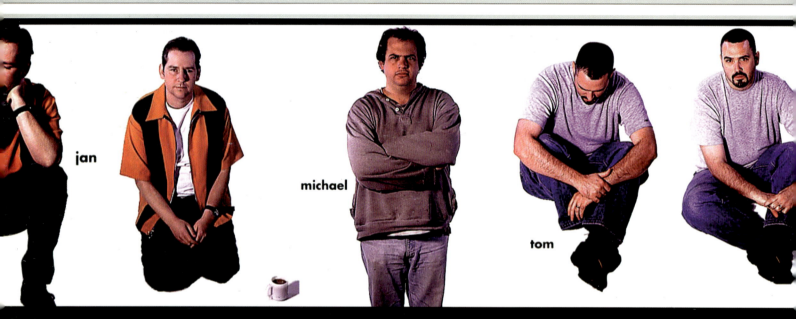

jan

michael

tom

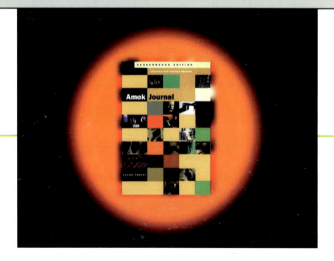

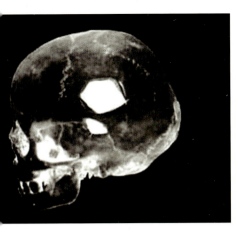

This horizontal image extends to great lengths and takes a long time to download. Only absolutely fascinating pages are worth taking so much time over.

mike

pathfinder.com/twep/Features/Delirium/

Delirium

(http://pathfinder.com/twep/Features/Delirium/)

The Delirium homepage, found in the Time-Warner Pathfinder, is the online version of a novel consisting of four stories (Drought, Magdala, Panopticon, and Anamnesis) with 21 chapters each. The vast amount of text overwhelmed me, and it is impossible to summarize the stories briefly. Browsing through the story, I could see that very great effort is required to create a site like this, and that every page should contain a significant amount of graphics.

On the menu page, there is a big world map, and the first sentences of 48 chapters are lined up and hooked up to their chapters. Here is where the creators made the most of electronic media, for we can see the tremendous difference between computer and print-- namely, a story on the Web can be followed in a non-linear structure. However, since the links are not networked from one page to another, it is hard to follow the behavior of a particular character in the story.

The writer, Douglas Cooper, was born in Canada, and has lived in Montreal, Paris, and London. He is a unique artist who has been wandering with his backpack and laptop computer for seven years. He now lives in New York and is kept busy writing more novels, contributing articles to magazines such as *Wired*, and participating in multimedia projects. It is nice to know that unique people like him exist. The interface was designed by Barry Deck, a highly respected font artist.

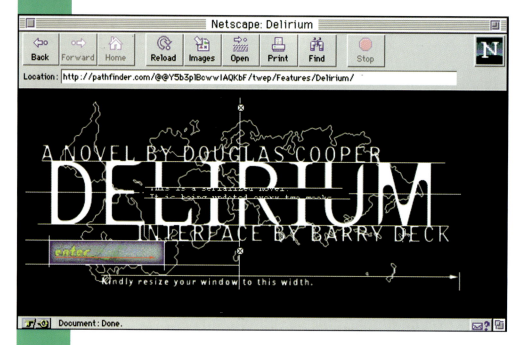

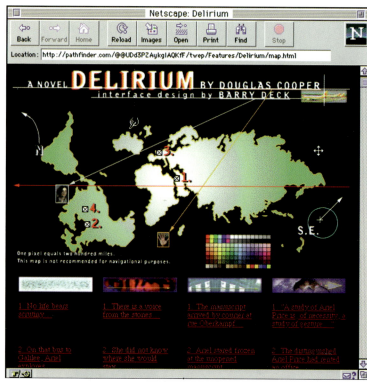

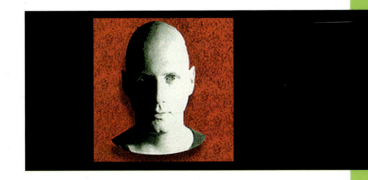

The homepage shows mainly text but also uses some sounds. Though the page, which appeared on the Web as early as 1994, was praiseworthy at that time, upon re-examination, I conclude that this type of presentation will not be effective in the future. It is time consuming to read so much text, and when sitting in front of a monitor, our attention span tends to be shorter than when sitting in a chair reading a book or watching television. Moreover, in front of a monitor, we expect interactive communication, even if it consists of nothing more than clicking a mouse. We do not want a one-way communication of receiving information from a screen. Developing a successful storytelling technique for interactive media will be a challenging and interesting endeavor.

www.asiaconnect.
com.my

Asia Connect

(http://www.asiaconnect.com.my)

I was surprised and excited when I met Asia Connect, the homepage built in Malaysia. Because in the past I have accessed homepages almost completely from Western English speaking countries, I was not at all familiar with Asian sites and had something of a prejudice against them, thinking they would be all too similar to Japan's in both design and technique.

However, when I encountered the technical and artistic refinement of Asia Connect's homepage, I realized how foolish my prejudice was and happily discarded it. In fact, now, while Japan is so absorbed by things like the infrastructure of networks and the vitality of the software industry, Asian countries are full of vigor and energy in the field of design, and I am afraid that they may get far ahead of us in the near future, with the one exception of animation.

Asia Connect's homepage is a kind of index of information about business, culture, campus, and coffee shop, etc., in Malaysia and other Southeast Asian Countries. Some pages are linked to other homepages, while a good number are still under construction. I look forward to seeing the treasure of information they will offer when they are completed.

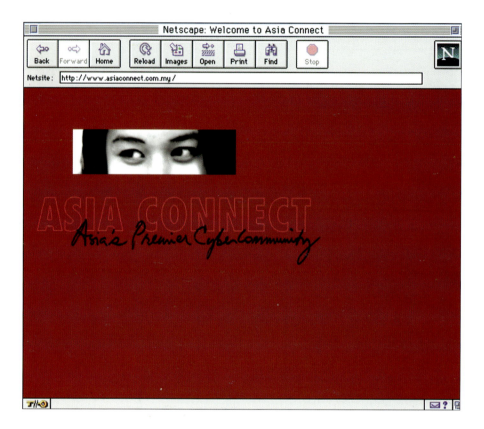

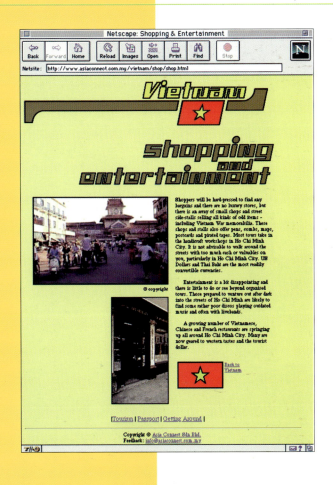

Netscape: Shopping & Entertainment

Netsite: http://www.asiaconnect.com.my/vietnam/shop/shop.html

Vietnam
shopping and entertainment

Shoppers will be hard-pressed to find any bargains and there are no luxury stores, but there is an array of small shops and street side-stalls selling all kinds of odd items - including Vietnam War memorabilia. These shops and stalls also offer peas, combs, maps, postcards and pirated tapes. Most tours take in the handicraft workshops in Ho Chi Minh City. It is not advisable to walk around the streets with too much cash or valuables on you, particularly in Ho Chi Minh City. US Dollars and Thai Baht are the most readily convertible currencies.

Entertainment is a bit disappointing and there is little to do or see beyond organised tours. Those prepared to venture out after dark into the streets of Ho Chi Minh are likely to find some rather poor discos playing outdated music and often with livebands.

A growing number of Vietnamese, Chinese and French restaurants are springing up all around Ho Chi Minh City. Many are now geared to western tastes and the tourist dollar.

Back to Vietnam

| Tourism | Passport | Getting Around |

Copyright © Asia Connect Sdn Bhd.
Feedback: info@asiaconnect.com.my

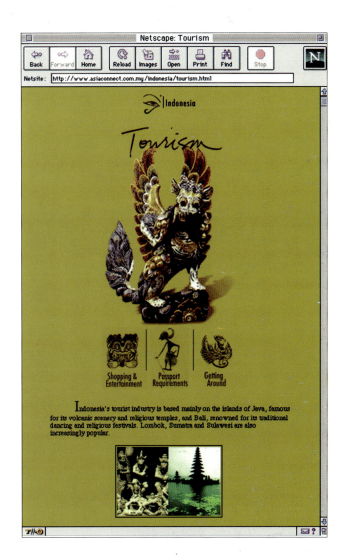

Netscape: Tourism

Netsite: http://www.asiaconnect.com.my/indonesia/tourism.html

Indonesia

Tourism

Shopping & Entertainment | Passport Requirements | Getting Around

Indonesia's tourist industry is based mainly on the islands of Java, famous for its volcanic scenery and religious temples, and Bali, renowned for its traditional dancing and religious festivals. Lombok, Sumatra and Sulawesi are also increasingly popular.

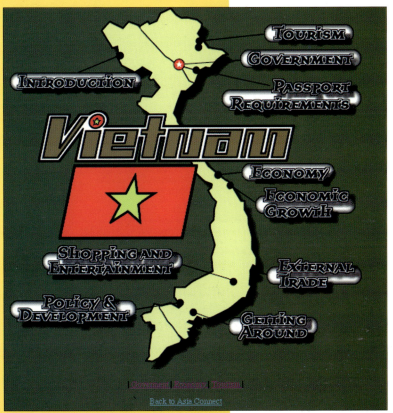

TOURISM
GOVERNMENT
PASSPORT REQUIREMENTS

Vietnam

ECONOMY
ECONOMIC GROWTH

EXTERNAL TRADE

GETTING AROUND

INTRODUCTION

SHOPPING AND ENTERTAINMENT

POLICY & DEVELOPMENT

| Government | Economy | Tourism |

Back to Asia Connect

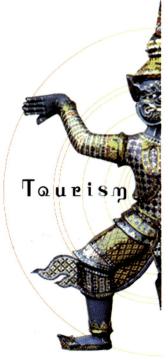

Tourism

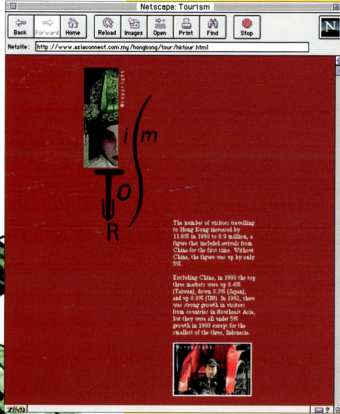

These are the front pages featuring Southeast Asian countries, which can each be distinguished by vivid background colors. The graphic components are all very exotic.

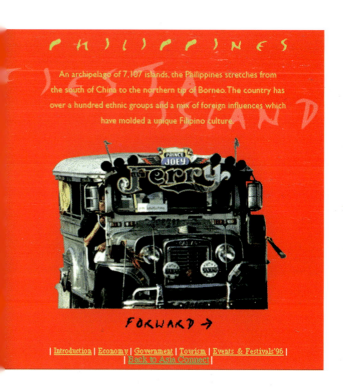

PHILIPPINES

An archipelago of 7,107 islands, the Philippines stretches from the south of China to the northern tip of Borneo. The country has over a hundred ethnic groups and a mix of foreign influences which have molded a unique Filipino culture.

FORWARD →

| Introduction | Economy | Government | Tourism | Events & Festivals'96 |
| Back to Asia Connect |

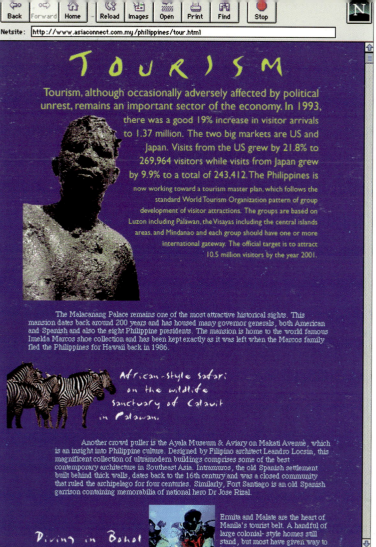

TOURISM

Tourism, although occasionally adversely affected by political unrest, remains an important sector of the economy. In 1993, there was a good 19% increase in visitor arrivals to 1.37 million. The two big markets are US and Japan. Visits from the US grew by 21.8% to 269,964 visitors while visits from Japan grew by 9.9% to a total of 243,412. The Philippines is now working toward a tourism master plan, which follows the standard World Tourism Organization pattern of group development of visitor attractions. The groups are based on Luzon including Palawan, the Visayas including the central islands areas, and Mindanao and each group should have one or more international gateway. The official target is to attract 10.5 million visitors by the year 2001.

The Malacanang Palace remains one of the most attractive historical sights. This mansion dates back around 200 years and has housed many governor generals, both American and Spanish and also the eight Philippine presidents. The mansion is home to the world famous Imelda Marcos shoe collection and has been kept exactly as it was left when the Marcos family fled the Philippines for Hawaii back in 1986.

African-style safari on the wildlife sanctuary of Calauit in Palawan.

Another crowd puller is the Ayala Museum & Aviary on Makati Avenue, which is an insight into Philippine culture. Designed by Filipino architect Leandro Locsin, this magnificent collection of ultramodern buildings comprises some of the best contemporary architecture in Southeast Asia. Intramuros, the old Spanish settlement built behind thick walls, dates back to the 16th century and was a closed community that ruled the archipelago for four centuries. Similarly, Fort Santiago is an old Spanish garrison containing memorabilia of national hero Dr Jose Rizal.

Ermita and Malate are the heart of Manila's tourist belt. A handful of large colonial-style homes still stand, but most have given way to

Diving in Bohol

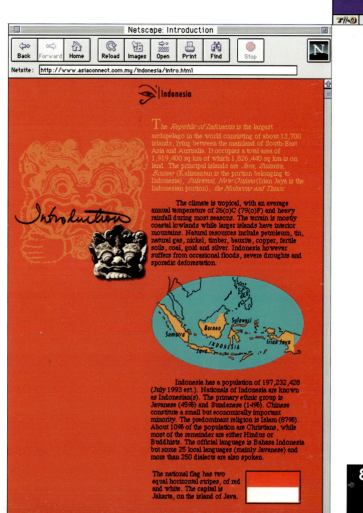

Indonesia

Introduction

The *Republic of Indonesia* is the largest archipelago in the world consisting of about 13,700 islands, lying between the mainland of South-East Asia and Australia. It occupies a total area of 1,919,400 sq km of which 1,826,440 sq km is on land. The principal islands are *Java, Sumatra, Borneo* (Kalimantan is the portion belonging to Indonesia), *Sulawesi, New Guinea* (Irian Jaya is the Indonesian portion), *the Moluccas and Timor.*

The climate is tropical, with an average annual temperature of 26(o)C (79(o)F) and heavy rainfall during most seasons. The terrain is mostly coastal lowlands while larger islands have interior mountains. Natural resources include petroleum, tin, natural gas, nickel, timber, bauxite, copper, fertile soils, coal, gold and silver. Indonesia however suffers from occasional floods, severe droughts and sporadic deforestation.

Indonesia has a population of 197,232,428 (July 1993 est.). Nationals of Indonesia are known as Indonesian(s). The primary ethnic group is Javanese (45%) and Sundanese (14%). Chinese constitute a small but economically important minority. The predominant religion is Islam (87%). About 10% of the population are Christians, while most of the remainder are either Hindus or Buddhists. The official language is Bahasa Indonesia but some 25 local languages (mainly Javanese) and more than 250 dialects are also spoken.

The national flag has two equal horizontal stripes, of red and white. The capital is Jakarta, on the island of Java.

Indonesia

Introduction Government Economy Tourism Events & Festivals

Get Shockwave Shockwave Indonesia

www.dircon.co.uk/lcf/ntouch.html

Ntouch Magazine

(http://www.dircon.co.uk/lcf/ntouch.html)

Design/Production Firm : The Web Lab.
Creative Director : Frank Rickett
Art Director : Fariba Farshad
Programmer : Hanafi Houbart
HTML Writers : Frank Rickett, Fariba Farshad

This U.K. web site is an online magazine featuring fashion and lifestyle created by young people studying fashion in London. The homepage shows various fashion scenes wit a radical atmosphere and the sensibility of the future trendsetters. Every page is highly colorful. rather than using the typical black or white background, the designers pasted large-format photographs onto a background of turquoise and pale purple. And they have incorporated the edge of the table tags into the design, which is not generally done because it tends to add seriousness to the pages. Just as in fashion design, they try to stay away from typical styles and ways of thinking, while at the same time avoiding a new-for-the-sake-of-being-new attitude that might result in designs in poor taste. In other words, they aim at a well-balanced sensitivity in all things.

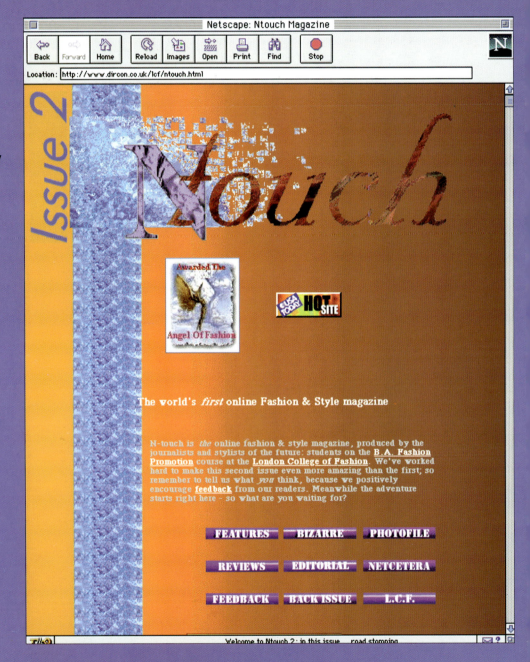

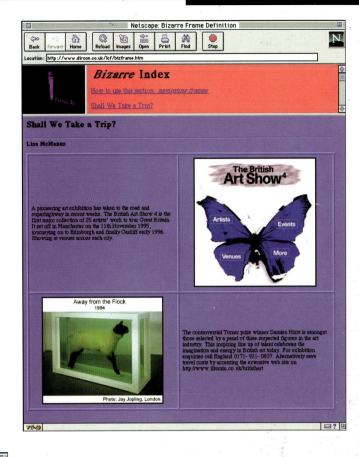

Netscape: Bizarre Frame Definition

Back Forward Home Reload Images Open Print Find Stop

Location: http://www.dircon.co.uk/lcf/bizframe.htm

Bizarre Index

How to use this section: *navigating frames*

Shall We Take a Trip?

Shall We Take a Trip?

Lisa McManus

A pioneering art exhibition has taken to the road and superhighway in recent weeks. The British Art Show 4 is the first major collection of 25 artists' work to tour Great Britain. It set off in Manchester on the 11th November 1995, journeying on to Edinburgh and finally Cardiff early 1996. Showing at venues across each city.

The British Art Show 4

Artists   Events

Venues   More

Away from the Flock
1994

Photo: Jay Jopling, London.

The controversial Turner prize winner Damien Hirst is amongst those selected by a panel of three respected figures in the art industry. This inspiring line up of talent celebrates the imagination and energy in British art today. For exhibition enquiries call England 0171- 921- 0837. Alternatively save travel costs by accessing the extensive web site on http://www.illumin.co.uk/britishart

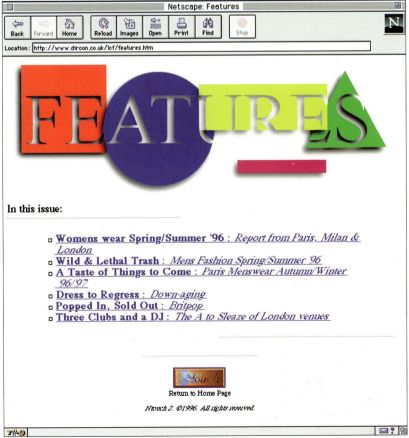

Netscape: Features

Back Forward Home Reload Images Open Print Find Stop

Location: http://www.dircon.co.uk/lcf/features.htm

FEATURES

In this issue:

- **Womens wear Spring/Summer '96** : *Report from Paris, Milan & London*
- **Wild & Lethal Trash** : *Mens Fashion Spring/Summer '96*
- **A Taste of Things to Come** : *Paris Menswear Autumn/Winter '96/'97*
- **Dress to Regress** : *Down-aging*
- **Popped In, Sold Out** : *Britpop*
- **Three Clubs and a DJ** : *The A to Sleaze of London venues*

Ntouch

Return to Home Page

Ntouch 2. ©1996. All rights reserved.

Frank Rickett

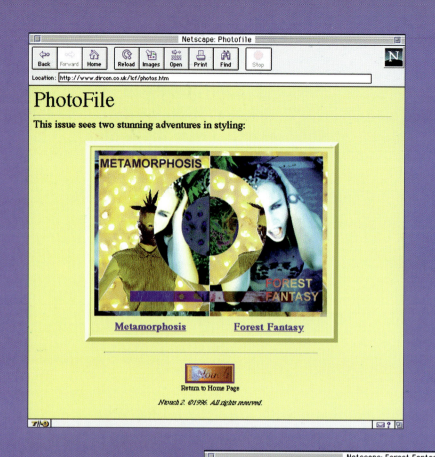

Location: http://www.dircon.co.uk/lcf/photos.htm

PhotoFile

This issue sees two stunning adventures in styling:

METAMORPHOSIS

FOREST FANTASY

Metamorphosis   **Forest Fantasy**

Return to Home Page

Ntouch 2. ©1996. All rights reserved.

Location: http://www.dircon.co.uk/lcf/bola.htm

Beetle devore velvet shawl, Owen Gaster. Pewter tiara, Slim Barrett, to order. Black suede mule, just seen, Emma Hope.

Cream textured wool dress, to order, Abe Hamilton. Brown distressed leather underbodice, Whitaker Malem, to order.

Chocolate/olive velvet shawl, Calver and Wilson. Chocolate devore velvet shift, John Rocha.

Beige leaf applique wool coat, Sonja Nuttall. Cream satin ballet shoes, Emma Hope, as before. Pewter crown, Slim Barrett.

MASARU MUTO

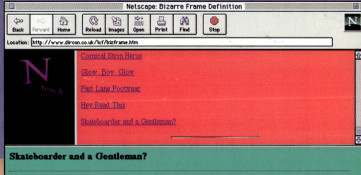

Netscape: Bizarre Frame Definition

Back Forward Home Reload Images Open Print Find Stop

Location: http://www.dircon.co.uk/lcf/bizframe.htm

N *touch*

Comical Strip Heros

Glow, Boy, Glow

Fast Lane Footwear

Hey Read This

Skateboarder and a Gentleman?

Skateboarder and a Gentleman?

INNOCENT SCRIBBLER

Hints of 'country casuals' have become evident among an unlikely street subculture. Skateboarders, traditionally untidy, rebellious young men denying adulthood, can now be seen sporting a discerning and all too sophisticated look in the name of fashion's latest fling. First spotted in Spring/Summer 95, the look is fast becoming part and Barbour of the new way to go in skating attire. Even companies like X-LARGE, FRESH, JIVE, DROORS and STUSSY are cashing in on the trend with new, sometimes witty takes on one time fashion no no's such as flat-caps, tank-tops, cardigans, and hounds-tooth patterned shirts in "old git" combinations of brown, khaki, creme and blue, trimmed with nautical or golfing emblems. Youch!

Although the days of obscene logo T-shirts expressing immature toilet humour are far from over, labels like FUCT, BITCH, and HOLMES have their work cut (should that be CUNT?) out, as more and more boarders abandon the obscene for the bespoke. Or at least bespoke with a well heeled, but decidedly ironic country dude's twist to it.

"I've got the funky fly golf gear from head to toe..." are the lyrics on Beastie Boys' album ILL COMMUNICATION, and this is the kind of cod-gent's gear band member and partner in X-LARGE Mike D, sports on stage. An action which appears to have encouraged a large portion of his skateboarding-audience to follow suite. Or Suit as the case seems to be. Plus-fours and a tweed blazer the natural progression in skateboarding attire? Who knows? But it's certainly an elegant look for all side-walk terrorists to make a dignified getaway in.

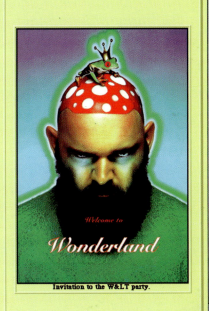

Netscape: A Taste of Things to Come...

Back Forward Home Reload Images Open Print Find Stop

Location: http://www.dircon.co.uk/lcf/parismen.htm

A Taste of Things to Come...

Nipped waists, slender silhouettes and techno-vibe fabrics, suggests a menswear season that's mixing the classic with the caustic to rule breaking effect, writes **Victor Benady**.

January 1996 and the fashion set are back in Paris again, this time for the Autumn/Winter 96-97 shows. Day one and we kick off with Naoki Takizawa for Issey Miyake who took the now familiar techno theme to an extreme. Shimmer synthetics were moulded using intricately laboured darts and seams to create a collection so glossy that it made your eyes bleed, culminating in silver quilted suits reflective enough to give the front row an opportunity to rearrange their hair. One thing was clear, Takizawa, one time design assistant for the company, has come of age, finding his own identity within the Miyake stable. Who better to massage your visual senses back into the land of the living than Paul Smith who mercilessly plugged le look anglais to our European neighbours. He delivered his usual repertoire of sleek tailoring in corduroy, velvet and eccentric plaids.

Expectations had put Walter Van Beirendonck at an immediate disadvantage. His latest backers, Mustang, forked out the money for yet another roller-coaster show production (about £300,000 to be precise) and all eyes were on him to at least equal the previous two W&LT super-collections. The message was clear: if you're going to see my show, you've got to really, really want to see my show. Of course, most people did, but after a half hour walk along a horse racing track towards a circus tent cleverly disguised as a toad stool, surrounded by fake snow (something they could have saved money on had they waited another day), most people had had that desire frozen out of them. Two and a half hours (including an hour and a half of delay), various Orchestre Symphonique Francais arrangements, and a serving of Shara Nelson later, there were some very disappointed faces leaving Walter's grotto. The clothes were clumsy and repetitive, hardly surprising seeing as Van Beirendonck has used up every possible "nice" permutation of colour combinations in his previous collections.

The W&LT party was that night but the thumping Belgian techno ensured that I got an early night. Thankfully so, if I was to make it to the John Rocha show at 9:30 the next morning - few did. Rocha added future elements of latex and laminates to velvet and tweed tailoring kept classically simple.

Invitation to the W&LT party.

The color and design, the eyes, the words "Welcome to Wonderland." Can we understand what these mean? It is an invitation card to a party given by the W&LT collection. The page at the left feature a report on the autumn and winter fashion shows for '96-'97. The page (top right) shows cheerful designs on skateboards. If you look closely, you can see an elaborately designed and painted illustraton.

87

www.atlas.organic.com

Atlas

(http://atlas.organic.com)

Client : @tlas Magazine
Production : @tlas Web Design
Art Director :
David Karam,Amy Francheschini ,Olivier Laude
Creative Director :
Olivier Laude,David Karam,Amy Francheschini
Copywriter : Olivier Laude ,Ken Coupland
Designer : Amy Francheschini,David Karam
Illustrator : Mike Bartalos,Tim Carroll,Thorina Rose
Photographer :
Olivier Laude,Catherine Karnow,Ed Kashi
Michael Yamashita,George Steinmetz
Karen Kasmauski,Matt Black
HTML Writer : Michael Macrone
Programmer : Michael Macrone,David Karam

This E-zines, a digital magazine launched in 1995, has been submitted from San Francisco, the mecca of multimedia production. The contents include four categories, photo, multimedia, design, illustration, and with its vast amount of information, we should be prepared to expect the unexpected.
The graphics show advanced techniques, especially succeeding in reproducing pages full of elaborated images.
" I Wonder Why: Experimental Interactive Single", which can be downloaded from the Gravitech page in the multimedia section has an acute social awareness that has tackled issues such as drug-abuse.

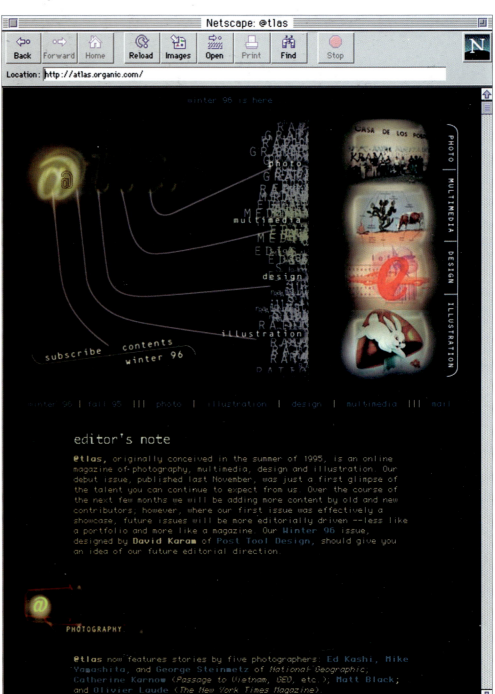

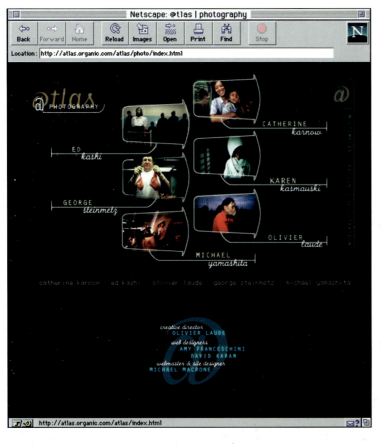

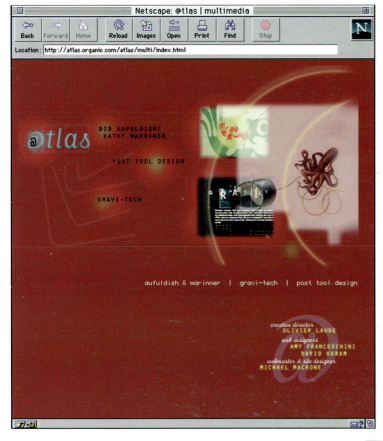

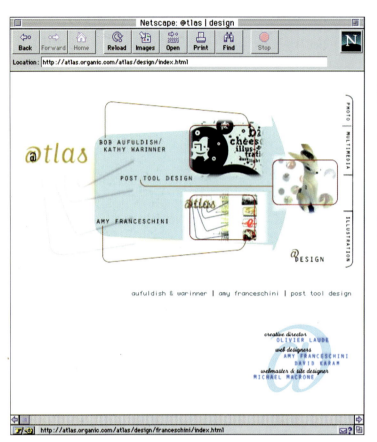

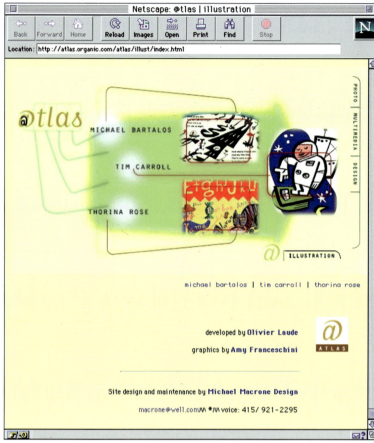

The design page (top) and the illustration page. (top right) The screen has a transparency, a soft atmosphere, and brilliant details. On the right side of the opposite page is a lengthy description of the activities of the designers, including the following: "The fall of '95 was a very eventful one, and unfortunately, we had very little chance to work on Atlas. We are evicted from our office and could not start working again until February '96 when Organic Online offered us a place to work."

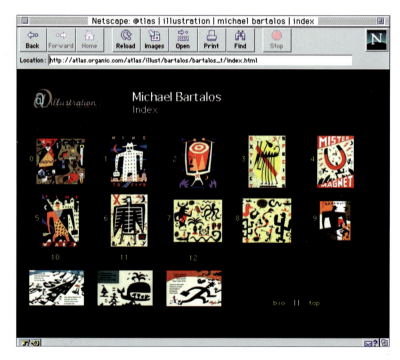

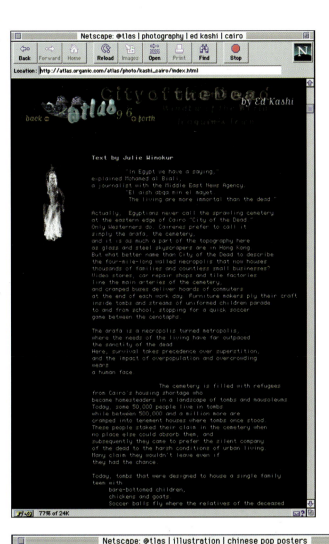

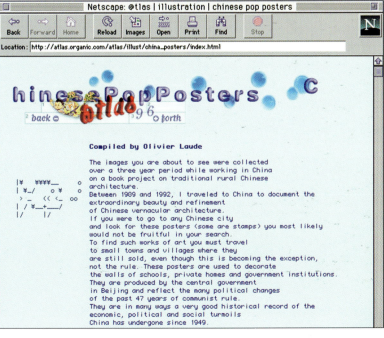

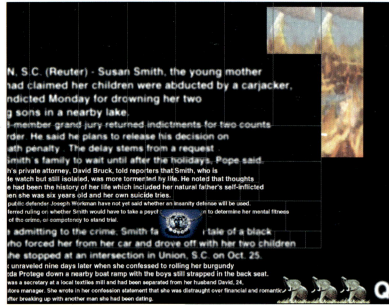

N, S.C. (Reuter) - Susan Smith, the young mother
had claimed her children were abducted by a carjacker,
ndicted Monday for drowning her two
g sons in a nearby lake.
-member grand jury returned indictments for two counts
rder. He said he plans to release his decision on
ath penalty. The delay stems from a request
Smith's family to wait until after the holidays, Pope said.
h's private attorney, David Bruck, told reporters that Smith, who is
de watch but still isolated, was more tormented by life. He noted that thoughts
e had been the history of her life which included her natural father's self-inflicted
en she was six years old and her own suicide tries.
public defender Joseph Workman have not yet said whether an insanity defense will be used.
ferred ruling on whether Smith would have to take a psych   n to determine her mental fitness
of the crime, or competency to stand trial.
e admitting to the crime, Smith fa   tale of a black
who forced her from her car and drove off with her two children
he stopped at an intersection in Union, S.C. on Oct. 25.
unraveled nine days later when she confessed to rolling her burgundy
da Protege down a nearby boat ramp with the boys still strapped in the back seat.
was a secretary at a local textiles mill and had been separated from her husband David, 24,
tore manager. She wrote in her confession statement that she was distraught over financial and romantic
after breaking up with another man she had been dating.

This is the MM director movie, "I Wonder Why".
The reason this section was named Experimental
Interactive Single is that, wherever you click on the
screen, you get back an audiovisual response. This
page can be downloaded from the GRAVI-TEC
page in the multimedia section.

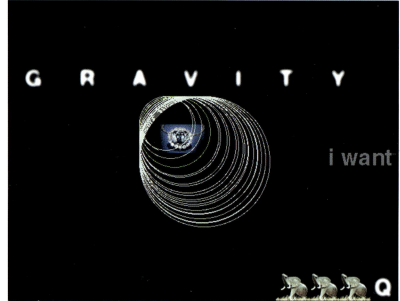

GRAVITY

i want

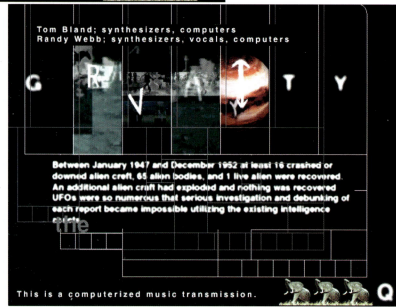

Tom Bland; synthesizers, computers
Randy Webb; synthesizers, vocals, computers

G R A V I T Y

Between January 1947 and December 1952 at least 16 crashed or
downed alien craft, 65 alien bodies, and 1 live alien were recovered.
An additional alien craft had exploded and nothing was recovered
UFOs were so numerous that serious investigation and debunking of
each report became impossible utilizing the existing intelligence

trie

This is a computerized music transmission.

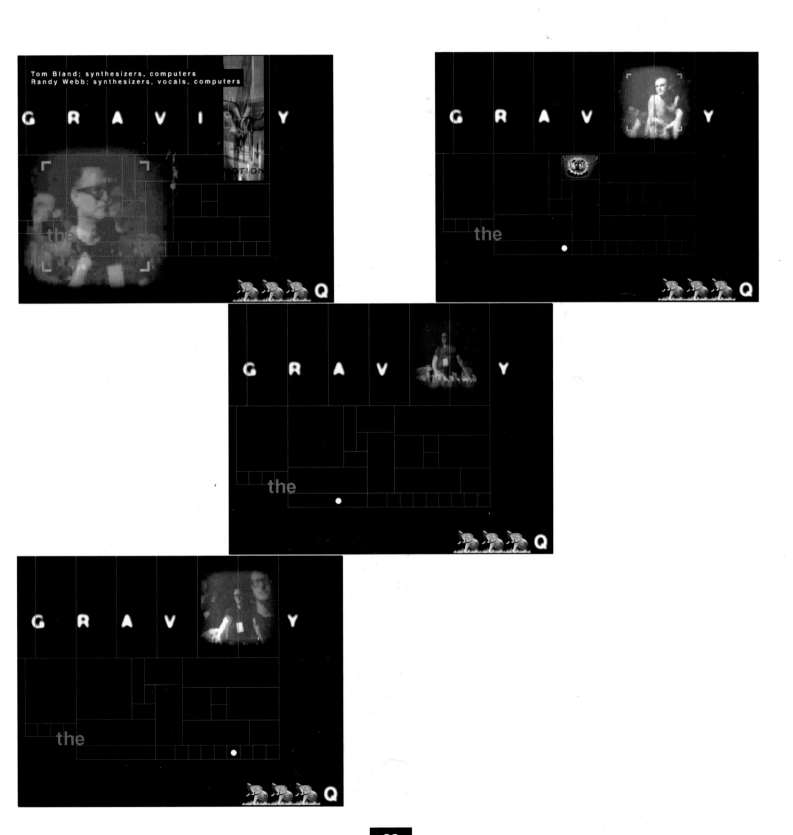

www.eLogic.com

eLogic

(http://www.elogic.com)

eLogic is a production company based in Venice, California. It specializes in creating web sites for advertising. Their site works both as a kind of information booklet introducing the company and as a showcase of the business. The design of the eLogic homepage is very fresh-looking, using mainly green against a black and white background. The screen icons on the elaborate back ground of the Kampah Visions' homepage in the Portfolio corner are very impressive, and the page also offers videos made by the company, some of which can be downloaded.

The resident of Kampah Vision is Flavio Kampah, an internationally renowned broadcaster and designer. The video archive on the homepage includes designs for well-known companies like Nexus, Cherry Coke, and Hyundai.

This is a monochrome photographic image shown on the Kampah Vision page. The skin head in the picture is Flavio Kampah, who, here, seems to look a bit like a philosopher.

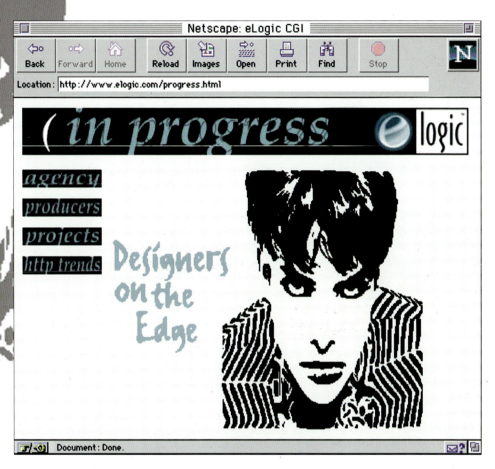

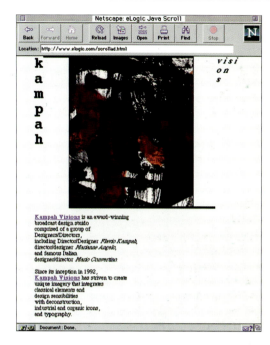

in progress (left) shows the experimental projects which the company is currently working on.
This page (top) shows a brief outline of Kampah Vision. Its main image creates the impression of a Chinese ink drawing.
This page (bottom left and right) shows a TV commercial film designed by the company.

www.jwtworld.com

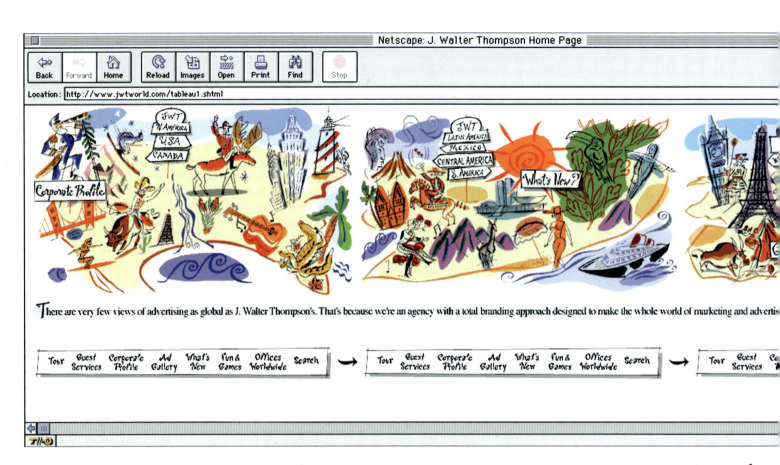

Location: http://www.jwtworld.com/tableau1.shtml

There are very few views of advertising as global as J. Walter Thompson's. That's because we're an agency with a total branding approach designed to make the whole world of marketing and advertisi

J.Walter Thompson WorldWide

(http://www.jwtworld.com)

This is the homepage for the international advertising agency, J. Walter Thompson. It serves as the company brochure. Despite the company's rather stiff image, it has designed a colorful and snappy homepage. We cannot help but admire it.

The front page is a menu constructed with a super-horizontal layout. Leaving aside any debate about whether this kind of layout is problematical, it undoubtedly has a strong impact on viewers. Many natural scenes and objects from all over the world are drawn on the page, and they impart the feeling that this, indeed, is a world wide business.

The contents are comprehensive, including a company profile, an introduction to its branch offices, an ad gallery displaying designs from some of the branches, and an amusement corner with a game section. The illustrations are so vibrant that we cannot help browsing all the way through to the last age.

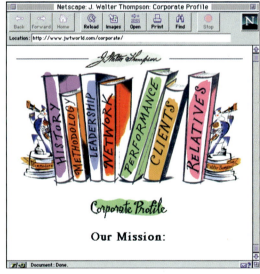

Click on Region of Interes

Browse at your leisure, or take our JWT World Tour. Either way, we'll give you everything you could want for your trip through our world. Except, of course, frequent flyer miles. (Like you need them anyway.)

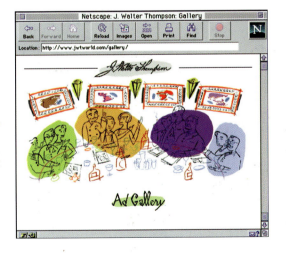

Predictably, the homepage is very unified and clearly shows the company's awareness of the importance of presentation. The illustrations look light and easygoing, but the unifying thread running throughout the site obviously required careful thought and planning. Many people were involved in designing the homepage, so the danger of too many cooks spoiling the broth was a real one. They were able to avoid that trap and maintain so clear a unity is especially noteworthy.

www.wowdigital.com

Wow Digital Imaging

(http://www.wowdigital.com)

Designer/Technical Director : Darrell Dingerson
Writer : Cleo Johnson
Creative Director : John Fezzuoglio

Though the homepage is based on a monotone image and at first sight seems to be somewhat tame, there are a good number of devices and a wide array of information, making for a good-looking site.

Upon accessing the page, an eye that looks into ours and the word " listen" pop up. Just seeing them creates a tension in us and makes us wonder what will happen next. Browsing through the page, however, I felt surprised that nothing much seemed to come up. "It can't be so," I thought, and so it wasn't. The icons used for linking are hidden on the page; on clicking one of them, the next information appears. There is an elaborate device that inserts the corresponding parts on the same page rather than linking them to another page, which is the ordinary way. It is extremely difficult to explain, but try to imagine a folding screen with many sections. If you look at when it is closed, you can see only the first and last section, but if you open it up, you can see the other parts. The image in the screen is similar to such a close-up folding screen, which, when you click on it, opens and the inner "panels" pop out. There are many inner panels, each containing highly refined artwork.

The icon that accesses the company profile, called shameless pitch, shows a very amusing, self-deprecating wit.

A homepage as sophisticated and creative as this is rarely encountered. I highly recommend it to anyone who wants to make a fabulous homepage or who likes experimenting or simply enjoys net surfing.

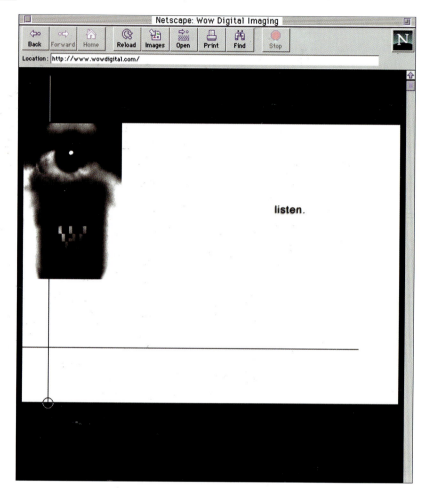

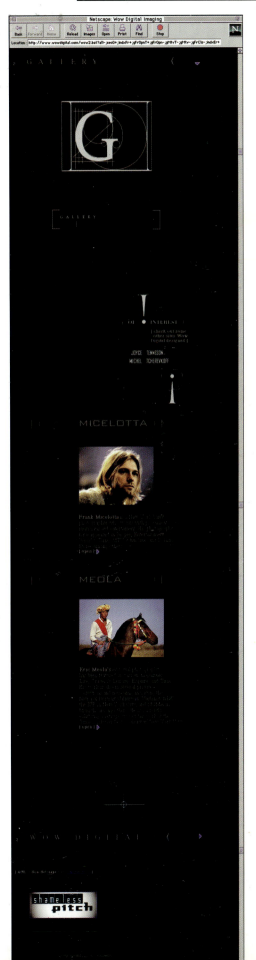

www.mediabridge.com/ fonthead/main.html

FONTHEAD DESIGN

Fonthead Design

(http://www.mediabridge.com/fonthead/main.html)

Design/Production Firm : Fonthead Design
Creative & Design : Ethan Dunham

This homepage uses soft coloring on a white background and is a showcase for the personal business of Ethan Dunham. A promising black and white image appearing at the top of every page hints of a good sense of humor. The homepage includes a number of interesting ages. There is one that gives advise on how to create your own.

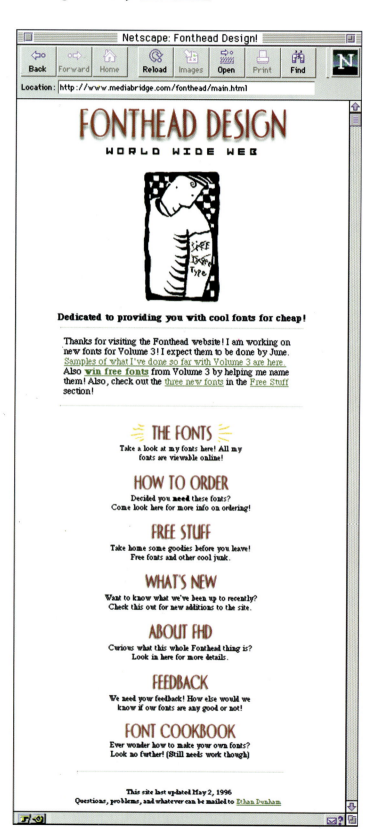

Allise
AaBbCcDdEeFfGgHhIiJjKk

ISEPIK
ABCDEFGHIJKLMNOPQ

BESSIE
ABCDEFGHIJKLM

JohnDoe
AaBbCcDdEeFfGgHhIiJjKk

Blearex
AaBbCcDdEeFfGgHhIiJjKk

MatrixDot
AaBbCcDdEeFfGgHhIiJjKk

BROIGA
ABCDEFGHIJKLMNOPQ

mekanek
abcdefghijklmnopqrs

Gritzpop
AaBbCcDdEeFfGgHhIiJjKk

MotherGoose
AaBbCcDdEeFfGgHhIiJjKk

GRITZPOP GRUNGE
ABCDEFGHIJKLMNOPQRSTUVWXYZ

ROCHESTER
ABCEFGHIJKLMNDP

Gurnsey
AaBbCcDdEeFfGgHhIiJjKk

Scrawl
AaBbCcDdEeFfGgHhIiJjKk

handskriptone
abcdefghijklmno

Sloppy Joe
AaBbCcDdEeFfGgHhIiJjKk

HolyCow
AaBbCcDdEeFfGgHhIiJjKk

SMITHPREMIER
ABCDEFGHIJKLMNOPQRSTUVWXYZ

HotCoffee
AaBBCCDDEEFFGGHHIiJjKK

TOUCAN GRUNGE
ABCDEFGHIJKLMNOPQRST

www.focus2.com

focus 2

(http://www.focus2.com)

focus 2 is a design company in Dallas. It is a *Communication Arts Magazine* award winner and works in both print and digital media. The homepage is a company brochure with a company outline and artwork. Its designs and devices are predictably very creative. One of its original designs consists of visuals with floating 3-D images set against a black background, and it has a mysterious beauty. The homepage has three sections : id, ego, superego. The use of terminology coined by Freud and the motif of 3-D images reflects the designers creativity. And many of their comments, especially in the philosophy and superego sections, show their open and playful personalities. The ego section includes a photographic tour page of the company. Their building was once the showroom for a car dealer, but when they took over, they redesigned it by creating a spacious and comfortable environment and then did the renovation themselves. Such motivation and energy is inspiring, but I'm jealous of them because I don't have it myself, while I do have a small, cramped office.

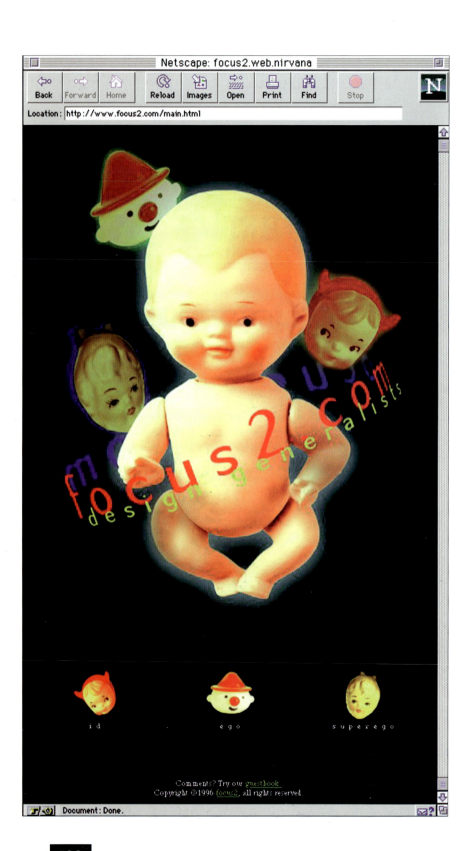

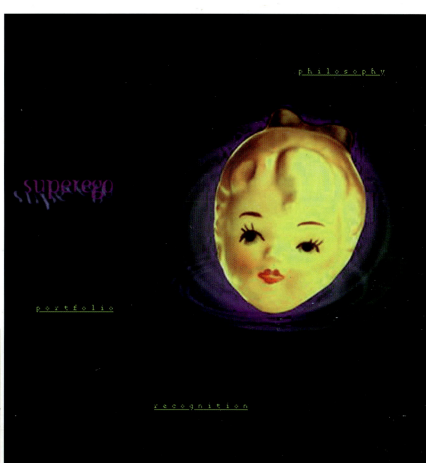

philosophy

superego

portfolio

recognition

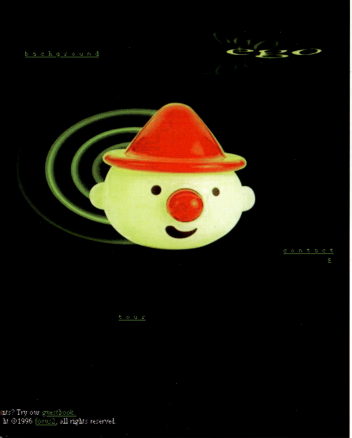

background

ego

contact
&

tour

www.cmdesigns.com

Clement Mok designs

(http://www.cmdesigns.com)

This is a San Francisco based design company that has recently (1996. April) changed its name to Studio Archetype. Its artwork includes the web sites mentioned above, Online (including user interface design for Microsoft Network), Branding Systems, Identity Systems, Packaging, Informationd Systems, New Media.

It has created web sites for Adobe, Sony, QVC, and others. They do all kinds of things, including the packaging designs for Nintendo Ultra 64 and a CI design for 3COM PARK, formerly Candlestick Park, home of the San Francisco Giants and the Forty-Niners, as well. The information can be accessed from the Case Studies section on the homepage. The Net Cafe section has essays on design by Clement Mok and data about 3-D chair, which can be downloaded, making this brochure more than just a company outline. The screen has a familiar design with a simple layout, colorful tool bars, and nice icons.

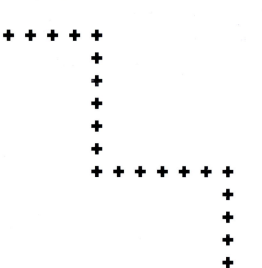

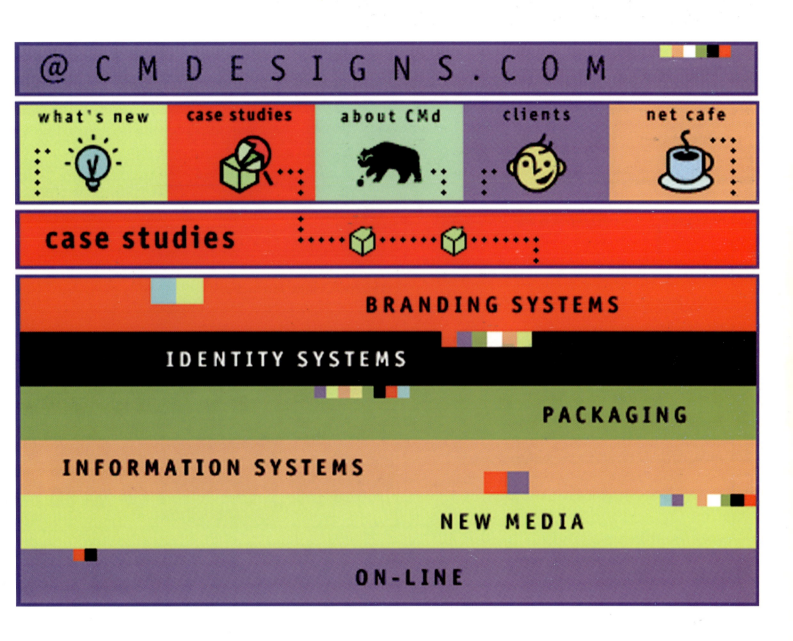

@ C M D E S I G N S . C O M

| what's new | case studies | about CMd | clients | net cafe |

case studies

BRANDING SYSTEMS

IDENTITY SYSTEMS

PACKAGING

INFORMATION SYSTEMS

NEW MEDIA

ON-LINE

This is a clickable image with charming icons. It is made up of a lot of colors but does not seem loud or noisy. The color blocks at the bottom of the page are linked to the corresponding section mentioned in each text.

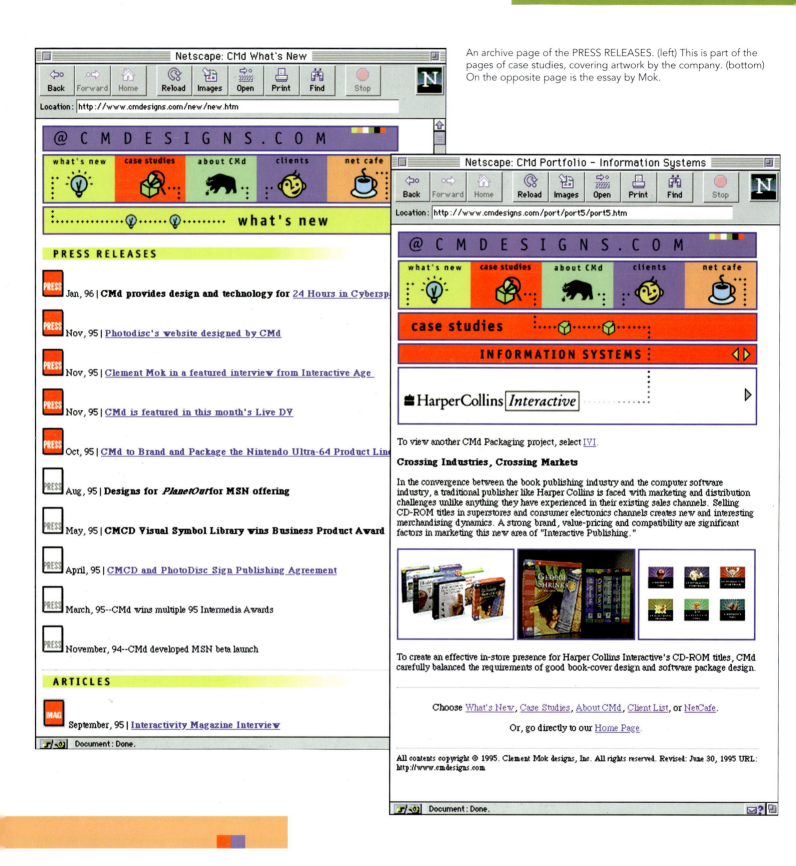

An archive page of the PRESS RELEASES. (left) This is part of the pages of case studies, covering artwork by the company. (bottom) On the opposite page is the essay by Mok.

Netscape: CMd What's New

Back | Forward | Home | Reload | Images | Open | Print | Find | Stop

Location: http://www.cmdesigns.com/new/new.htm

@ C M D E S I G N S . C O M

what's new | case studies | about CMd | clients | net cafe

what's new

PRESS RELEASES

PRESS Jan, 96 | **CMd provides design and technology for** 24 Hours in Cybersp[ace]

PRESS Nov, 95 | Photodisc's website designed by CMd

PRESS Nov, 95 | Clement Mok in a featured interview from Interactive Age

PRESS Nov, 95 | CMd is featured in this month's Live DV

PRESS Oct, 95 | CMd to Brand and Package the Nintendo Ultra-64 Product Lin[e]

PRESS Aug, 95 | **Designs for** *PlanetOut* **for MSN offering**

PRESS May, 95 | **CMCD Visual Symbol Library wins Business Product Award**

PRESS April, 95 | CMCD and PhotoDisc Sign Publishing Agreement

PRESS March, 95--CMd wins multiple 95 Intermedia Awards

PRESS November, 94--CMd developed MSN beta launch

ARTICLES

MAG September, 95 | Interactivity Magazine Interview

Document: Done.

Netscape: CMd Portfolio - Information Systems

Back | Forward | Home | Reload | Images | Open | Print | Find | Stop

Location: http://www.cmdesigns.com/port/port5/port5.htm

@ C M D E S I G N S . C O M

what's new | case studies | about CMd | clients | net cafe

case studies

INFORMATION SYSTEMS

HarperCollins *Interactive*

To view another CMd Packaging project, select IVI.

Crossing Industries, Crossing Markets

In the convergence between the book publishing industry and the computer software industry, a traditional publisher like Harper Collins is faced with marketing and distribution challenges unlike anything they have experienced in their existing sales channels. Selling CD-ROM titles in superstores and consumer electronics channels creates new and interesting merchandising dynamics. A strong brand, value-pricing and compatibility are significant factors in marketing this new area of "Interactive Publishing."

To create an effective in-store presence for Harper Collins Interactive's CD-ROM titles, CMd carefully balanced the requirements of good book-cover design and software package design.

Choose What's New, Case Studies, About CMd, Client List, or NetCafe.

Or, go directly to our Home Page.

Document: Done.

CORE

(http://www.core77.com:80)

This site carries a lot of information about the design field. Core 77, Inc. specializes in multimedia development, such as CD-ROMs and Information Kiosks. Various essays on digital design appear on the site and they provide substantial reading.]Incidentally, Core 77, Inc. designed the graphic parts of Auto Desk.

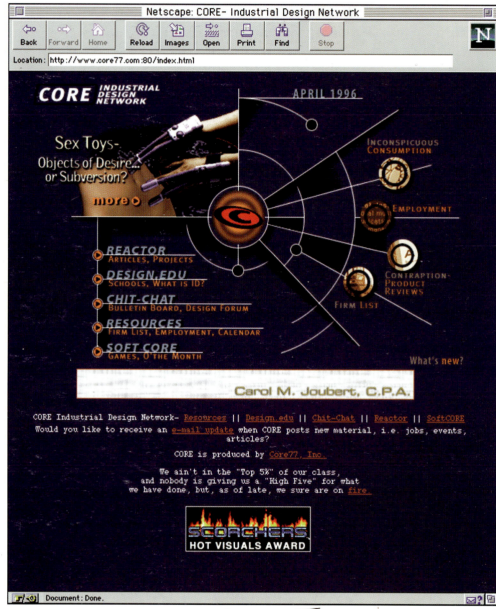

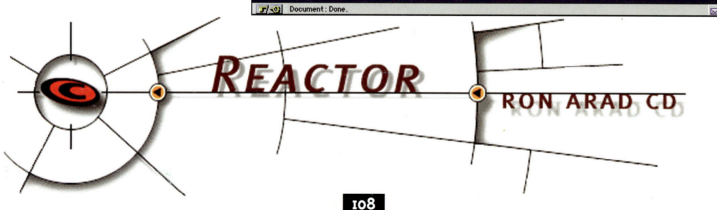

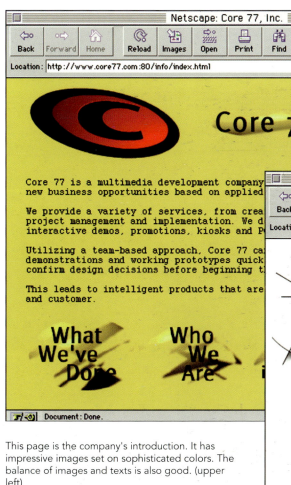

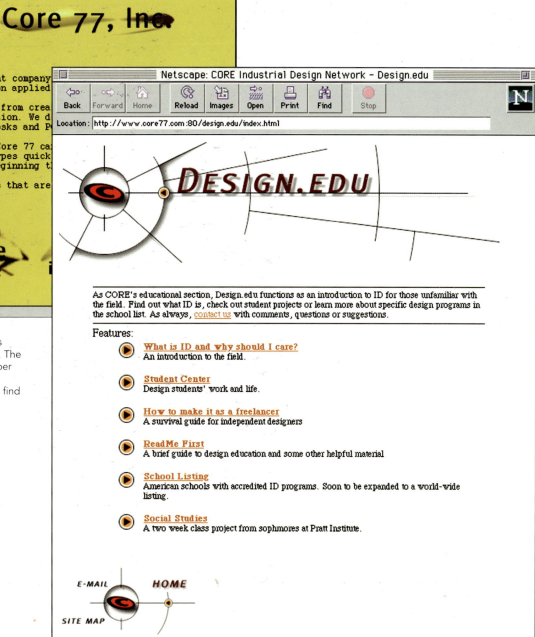

This page is the company's introduction. It has impressive images set on sophisticated colors. The balance of images and texts is also good. (upper left)

This section is "DESIGN.EDU", where you can find essays about the designers. (right)

rampages.onramp.net/ ~dreier

Dreier Design

(http://rampages.onramp.net/~dreier)

Design/Production Firm : Dreier Design
Client : Self
Art Director : Kyle D. Dreier
Creative Director : Kyle D. Dreier
Copywriter : Kyle D. Dreier
Designer : Kyle D. Dreier
Illustrator : Kyle D. Dreier
Photographer : Mark Bumgarner
HTML Writer : Kyle D. Dreier
Programmer : Kyle D. Dreier
Other : Deanna Schneider (Creative Assistant)

The site places emphasis on "simple is beautiful" (does that sound rather old-fashioned?). The site takes the typical style of a designer's online portfolio; it uses the white background as a sketch book and places its own works on display. Identity, collateral, illustration, editorial, misc/etc. are sections that show us past achievements in each field. The visual images are clean.
The provider, Kyle Dreier is a young designer mainly active in the printing industry. He has won several prizes from *Communication Arts, How,* etc.

The menu consists of
16 square images
designed with pictures
and types. (page110)
An illustration for the
film festival in
Colorado. (bottom)
The promotional desk
calenders of American
Airlines. (right)

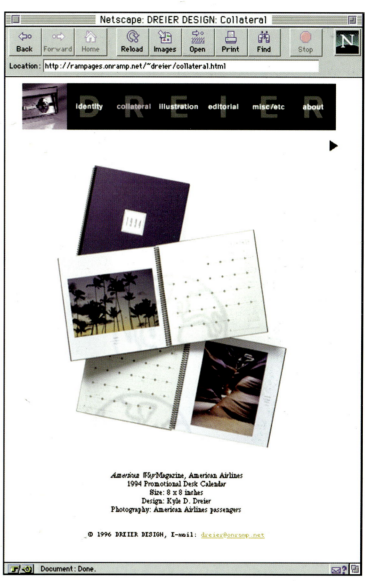

Netscape: DREIER DESIGN: Collateral

Location: http://rampages.onramp.net/~dreier/collateral.html

identity collateral illustration editorial misc/etc about

American Way Magazine, American Airlines
1994 Promotional Desk Calendar
Size: 8 x 8 inches
Design: Kyle D. Dreier
Photography: American Airlines passengers

© 1996 DREIER DESIGN, E-mail: dreier@onramp.net

Document: Done.

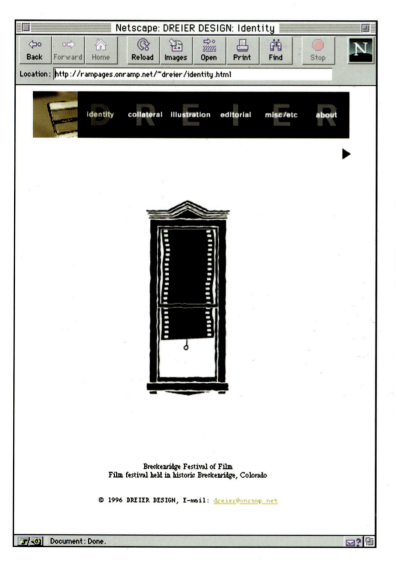

Netscape: DREIER DESIGN: Identity

Location: http://rampages.onramp.net/~dreier/identity.html

identity collateral illustration editorial misc/etc about

Breckenridge Festival of Film
Film festival held in historic Breckenridge, Colorado

© 1996 DREIER DESIGN, E-mail: dreier@onramp.net

Document: Done.

www.rezn8.com

ReZ.n8 Production

(http://www.rezn8.com)

Rez.n8 Production specializes in SFX and animation titles for film companies. Recently, it has also begun the construction of web sites, for example, Disney Channel, Fox Sports and Apple Multimedia Program. Reflecting its career as a design company, this home page, which also functions as a guide to Rez.n8 Production, is full of innovative visual techniques. From the very beginning of the page, for example, a slide (projector) show by the server push rushes out and goes on to represent past works in succession. Although the site does not give us much sense of speed, it is still visually impressive and deserves viewing. Once you step into it, topics like us, services, clients, ideas unfold on black and white pages with twisted icons. Here, it shows us its attachment to visualization. In homepage designing, indication of text can thus far only be controlled on the client computer side, but here, when the user wishes to indicate letters as he pleases visually, these letters are transformed into graphic images. Compared to text data, it takes longer to transmit the information, but it enables the user to control the images. Rez.n8 Production seems to be concentrating on an exhaustive study on this issue in its site.

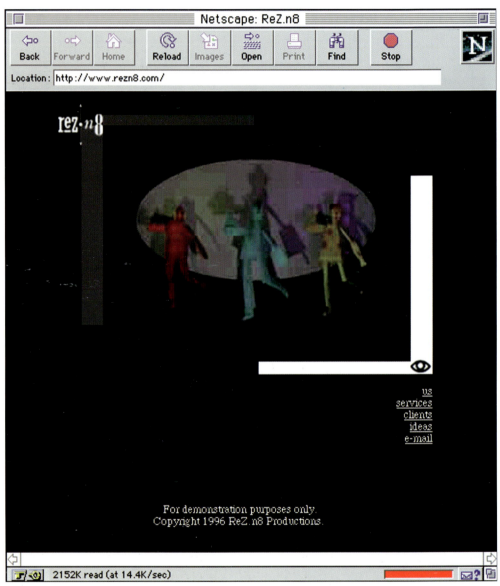

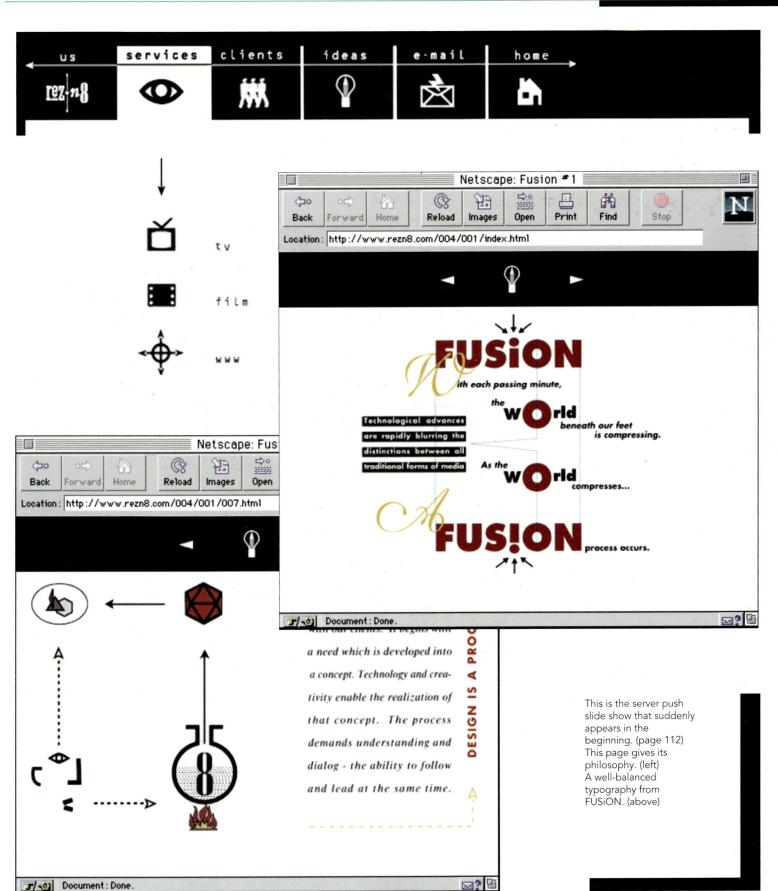

This is the server push slide show that suddenly appears in the beginning. (page 112) This page gives its philosophy. (left) A well-balanced typography from FUSiON. (above)

www.lavamind.com

LavaMind®

LavaMind

(http://www.lavamind.com)

Design/Production Firm : LavaMind
Art Director : Naomi Kokubo
Creative Director : Steven Hoffman
Designer : Steven Hoffman
Illustrator: Naomi Kokubo
HTML Writer : Naomi Kokubo
Programmer : Steven Hoffman

Lava Mind is a game-creator team from San Fransisco formed by Naomi Kokubo and Steven Hoffman. Zapitalism and the Archipelago of Mermadan, Gazillionaire and the Galaxy of Gogg, Virtual Pet Cemetery, Lunatic Landing on the West Side are some of the bizarre titles in its site, and the humorous, but slightly peculiar illustrations of its characters, attract the attention of many net-surfer. Not only are the characters attractive, but the contents are, too. For example, The Virtual Pet Cemetery carries articles contributed by pet enthusiasts with lots of posing for effect. You can see that this is not just another homepage by a game creator. I know that the logo images such as Top5% of Point and Three Stars of Magellan are found on popular home pages. So, it is perhaps a little surprising that there is a Pet Lovers Association Honor List in this section. Enthusiastic pet lovers seem to be everywhere.
This team has also done some CD-ROM games, one of which, a trial demo of the Gazillionaire can be downloaded.

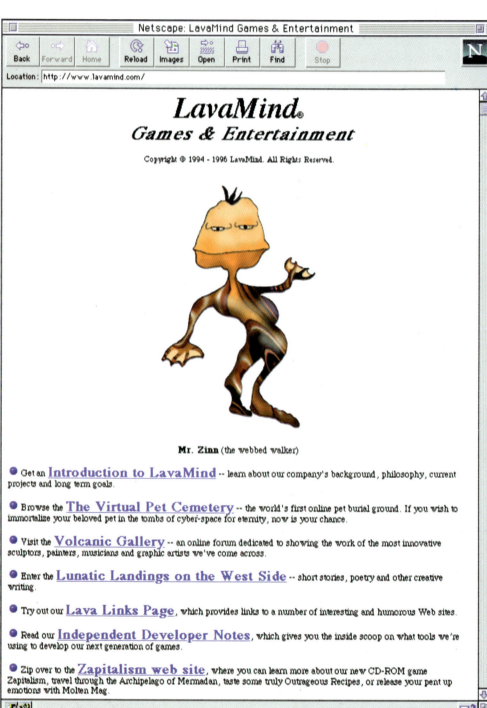

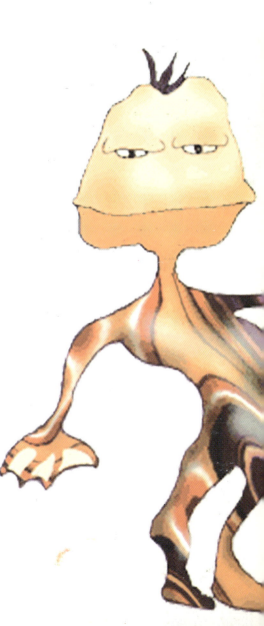

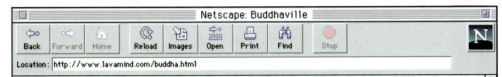

Netscape: Buddhaville

| Back | Forward | Home | Reload | Images | Open | Print | Find | Stop |

Location: http://www.lavamind.com/buddha.html

Buddhaville

by
Steven Hoffman

I stepped up onto the embankment and looked down over the tranquil, temperate, self-nurturing valley town. The sprawling grasslands brushed up against the shallow mountains and fell back onto slabs of tomato fields, green belts, flat frame houses, mothers who prayed for the PTA, children who worried about the environment, fathers who bicycled to work and pressured the city council to protect their precious utopia from the big city developers, clean frosted streets, well organized schools, dog houses, jungle gyms, and a population instilled with a compulsory sense of civic devotion.

As the morning sun shifted high over the valley warming the stagnant creek at the far edge of town and sending trickles of sweat down the backs of the migrant workers laboring in the fields, the self styled suburban neighborhoods slowly came to life. However, unlike any other day, there was a subtle tension stretching through the sinews of residential blocks, across the faces of the children as they made their way to school, down into the soil of the well fertilized lawns, and through the hearts of the timorous shop owners.

Something had changed while I was away. The town was no longer secure, self-justifying, hermetically sealed off from the rest of the world. It had been infected. A disease now lingered in the dark corners of each house, under the eucalyptus trees which lined 1st and 3rd streets, on the playgrounds, at the schools, and within the consciousness of every citizen. It was a disease which unmercifully bent the well preserved mental equilibrium the inhabitants had cultivated for so many years.

My eyes scanned the deliberately pacified landscape as I searched for the source of this sickness. On the railroad tracks at the base of the incline where I stood were several men wearing blue jackets and carrying rifles. They judiciously probed through clumps of tangled undergrowth, overturned empty wooden crates, and peered into the abandoned freight cars.

Almost instantaneously, a commotion seemed to spread through the town. People were moving everywhere. Next to me appeared a young woman, her blond hair perfectly designed to tumble across her shoulders accenting her lemon lipstick and cherry red scarf. I studied her face. Slowly the disease began to seep from her lips, dribble down her well formed chin, and disperse into the air. As my lungs filled with her breath, I realized the true source of this disease: fear.

www.ideograf.com

Ideograf Creative
(http://www.ideograf.com)

Ideograf Creative is a company that specializes in such digital media designing as web site developing and CD-ROM authoring. Its homepage is an online brochure-a guide to the company composed with icons, typographies and neutral tinted backgrounds. The site is divided into four sections: crown, fire, wheel, ink. Each section introduces the production and staff (crown), past achievements (fire), a message board for the Viewers (wheel) and the experimental showcases (ink). ink, for example, has a slide show by the client pull (= an autonomous device that automatically renews its own pages), and entertains viewers with colorful graphic images and messages. Furthermore, when you click a basket ball icon, one of these images in the page entitled "In memory of Joshua 'Jo Jo' White", it is a tribute paid to the memory of the 23 year social worker, who was killed in Jan. 1994, introducing his poem. The intelligent phrases on the first pages of each section and on pages like above express the designers' messages very appropriately.

crown

fire

wheel

ink

home

search

email

AYODELE SELIGMAN HOMBRE
(man)
ayodele seligman

Art Director Ayodele Seligman is a graduate of design from the UCLA School of Arts. While at UCLA he was Assistant Art Director of The Daily Bruin, the second largest daily in Los Angeles. Ayodele has freelance experience working with ad agencies and design firms. He also art directed and designed a new media title and identity system for Ambient Digital Publishing. Most recently he was Art Director at Cybersight, a World Wide Web developer in Portland, Oregon.

i am art director.

my name comes from the Yoruba tribe in Nigeria

it means
JOY COMES HOME

i feel that the primal energy of this prehistoric pictogram represents my

creative flow

ideograf

The self introductory page of Ayodele Seligman, Art Director. It starts with his message "My name comes from the Yoruba tribe in Nigeria".
The images are full of earth colors and might be related to this. (above)

crown

www.duffy.com

duffy Design

(http://www.duffy.com)

Duffy Design, which operates this site, is originally a design studio that takes an active parts in various fields. Its clients include Armani, Coca-Cola, Rollerbrade and Ameritec. Its design is visually oriented using many illustrations. Its icons and colors are at once simple but sophisticated. The same could be said for its content-simple and sophisticated, and again, giving general information on its studio work.

These designers are not trying to become famous for elaborate home pages. This simplicity of the design seems to say that designing it is as easy as making a company signboard.

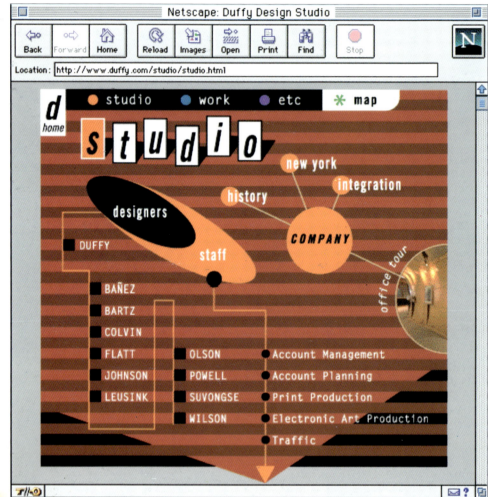

The clickable map image that introduces its business, from the corporate and brand IDs to the packages and printed matter. (above)

www.prophetcomm.com

Prophet Communications

(http://www.prophetcomm.com)

Design/Production Firm : Prophet Communications
Creative Director : Josh Feldman
Programmer : Jason Monberg
Others : Thor Muller (Executive Producer)

The most important thing for the graphics on a web site is to make such a deep visual impression that the viewers cannot help traveling the whole site. A trip to Prophet Communications shows us how important this is. That is, the graphics on Prophet Communication. Those are so unique and superior that viewers are compelled to linger. As they are slowly taken into its depth, they experience a trip into the stormy sea of colors and shapes. What becomes clear, then, is the strong presence of the creator, Josh Feldman, a computer wizard at hypermedia, who has created this site by himself. It is one of the most stimulating sites now on the Web.

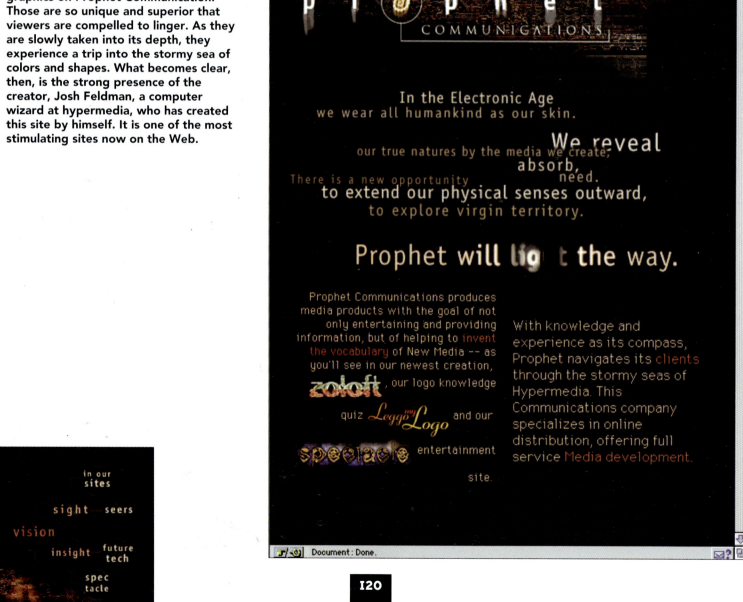

speciacle
PRESENTS
A PROPHET COMMUNICATIONS
PRODUCTION

zoloft

People living in churches
lead warped lives...
The zoloft initiation awaits you.

For the full zoloft experience, Netscape 2.0 and Shockwave are required.
For all other users, go to the universal version.

PROBLEMS? OUT OF MEMORY ERRORS?
ZOLOFT TECH SUPPORT IS READY TO ANSWER ALL YOUR QUESTIONS.

FOR INFO CONTACT: INFO@PROPHETCOMM.COM   ZOLOFT © 1996 PROPHET COMMUNICATIONS

Savor more Prophet content at the Spectacle Entertainment Page

INSIGHT

FUTURE TECH

SPECTACLE 4

www.iconomics.com

Iconomics®
The Global Illustration Resource

Iconomics

(http://www.iconomics.com)

This site, a witty coining from the words: icon and economics, is operated by a company with the same name, specializing in illustration and icon-design for professional design productions. Naturally, the highlights of the site here are the illustrations and icons. The site also serves as a showcase for the company's images and offers a series of outstanding illustrations. Moreover, if the viewer finds any favorite images from the site, online delivery is available. Although icons might seem to be unimportant components of a homepage, they are, in fact, essential for the overall impression of the site. Those who cannot draw cannot make beautiful icons, and their skill is rarely improved even when using a computer. And, too, sites that offer free icons or illustrations seldom offer anything really good. So, you can see that Iconomics is a real find. Do try some of their stylish images!

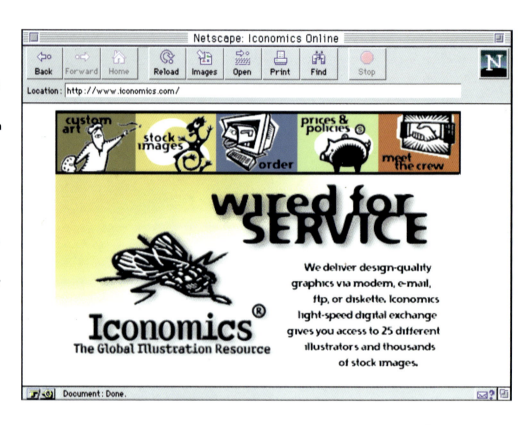

AB0A0001S AB0A0002S AB0A0003S AB0A0004S AB0A0005S

AB0A0006S AB0A0007S AB0A0008S AB0A0009S AB0A0010S

AB0A0011S AB0A0012S AB0A0013S AB0A0014S AB0A0015S

AB0A0016S AB0A0017S AB0A0018S AB0A0019S AB0A0020S

Back | Forward | Home | Reload | Images | Open | Print | Find | Stop

Location: http://www.iconomics.com/naOa/index.html

stock IMAGES

If you're on a tight budget or sweating another unrealistic deadline, call Iconomics. We will research and e-mail or fax you stock art linesheets from any of our artists. It's fast and best of all it could save you money!

Neal Aspinall

NA0A0001S   NA0A0002S   NA0A0003S   NA0A0004S   NA0A0005S

NA0A0006S   NA0A0007S   NA0A0006S   NA0A0008S

NA0A0010S   NA0A0011S   NA0A0012S   NA0A0013S

NA0A0014S   NA0A0015S   NA0A0016S   NA0A0017S   NA0A0018S

see custom art by this artist

WARNING: Custom Art takes a long time to download!

[Custom Art] [Stock Images] [Order] [Meet the Crew] [Prices & Policy] [Home]

ORDER

To contact your Iconomics representative call us at 1.800.297.7655, fax us at 1.303.493.6997 or use the electronic form below.

prices & POLICIES

Custom illustration for as little as $125 per image. Thousands of stock images starting at $55.

meet the CREW

Erik Hunter
tech specialist

Angela Sipe
operations manager

Richard Askew
creative manager

www.digiplanet.com

Digital Planet

(http://www.digiplanet.com)

Design/ProductionFirm : Digital Planet
Design Director : Michael Lenahan
Creative Director : Thomas Lakeman
Copywriter : Peter Kleiner, Stefan Grunspan
Designer : Scott Ford
HTMLWriter : Robert Balmaseda, Jenifer Greer
Programmer : Tamara Coombs, Jeff DeAnda

As you can guess by the name, this is the homepage of the web site team, which has dealt with such Hollywood productions as Casper and Apollo 13. GIFs with graduated color schemes are used for the backgrounds on every pages. These sensitive patterns can only be put into practice by downloading, which takes some time. Leaving aside the question of the benefit of creating pages with such large memory size, this site, unlike many typical ones, will certainly appeal to those who are not satisfied with run-of-the-mill design.

www.dol.com

designOnline

(http://www.dol.com)

Design/Production Firm :
bYte a tree (a division of STELLAR ViSIONs)
Client : designOnline, Inc.
Art Director : Stella Gassaway / bYte a Tree
Creative Director : Peter Fraterdeus / designOnline
Copywriter : bYte a tree / designOnline team
Designer : Stella Gassaway / bYte a Tree
Illustrator : Stella Gassaway / bYte a tree
digital choreographer : Gerry Mathews / bYte a tree
HTML Writer : bYte a tree
Programmer : Peter Fraterdeus / designOnline
Others : K. Swarner, M. Anderson, A. Mathews

This homepage mode by designOnline, Inc. is divided into four sections: dezinCafe, Design Compass, DOLinc, Marketplace. dezinCafe, in particular, has many topics of design and furnishes much useful information for professional designers and beginning enthusiasts alike.

dig+!

(http://www.and.or.jp/~dig)

Design/Production Firm : Degital Image Graphics(DIG+!)
Art Director : Tomohiko Matsumoto
Creative Director : Eisuke Shinkawa
Copywriter : Yutaro Oka
Designer : Eisuke Shinkawa
Photographer : Keiko Maeda
HTML Writer : Eisuke Shinkawa
Programmer : Tadahiro Shimizu, Eisuke Shinkawa
Others : Planning DIG+!

This is the homepage of dig (Digital Image Graphics, Inc.) , a young creative team from Tokyo. It introduces their manifest, their business guide and their own online magazine, DIGOUT. Its coloring and typography are somewhat similar to those of such independent magazines as *Bafaout.* On the whole, the structure of the site may strike viewers as uneven and naïve, but this is one of the most promising forces from Japan in terms of Tokyo street culture.

www.web.kyoto-inet.or.jp/org/grvito

GROOVISIONS
a web dealing with powers of groovisions

Groovisions

(http://www.web.kyoto-inet.or.jp/org/grvito)

Design/Production Firm : groovisions

High-speed, up-to-date Shockwave movies are often loaded into this site by the Kyoto-based artists. Its electronic mail news advises viewers about changes and renewal of the site and about events conducted by its own club.

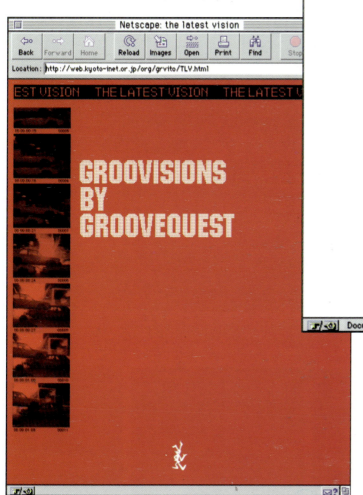

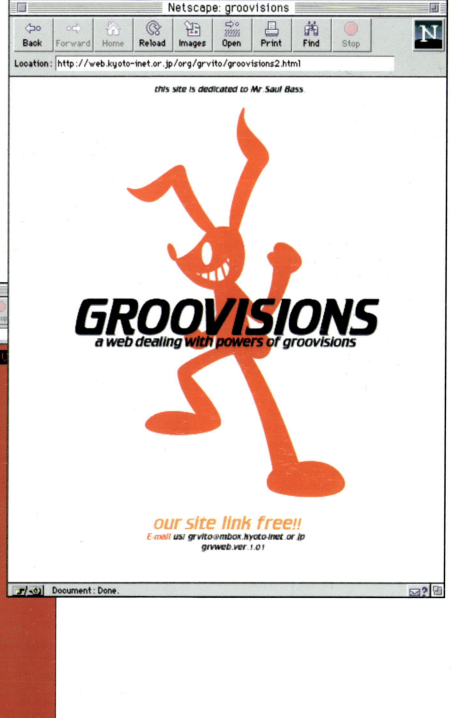

www.bradjohnson.com

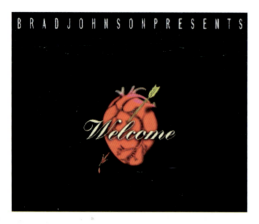

Brad Johnson Presents

(http://www.bradjohnson.com)

As soon as you access this site, the image of a throbbing heart (GIF animation) suddenly comes into view, and it is only the first sign of the drama within. This is a superb site full of unique ideas, building up a metaphorical and theatrical stage on its pages. project, gallery, biography and arcade are the four divisions of the site and these can be linked up to each page. Any information, recalled from the menu, is exhibited on the stage, and the authors' past achievements and biographies also appear. The graphics are very beautiful and of high quality. In addition, the micro-media movie, PINCH, which can be down loaded from the director's biography has been given a prize for its superiority. The whole thing is a good example of a highly creative individual site full of tricks and interesting ideas. Such as these are not often found in the web sites of major companies.

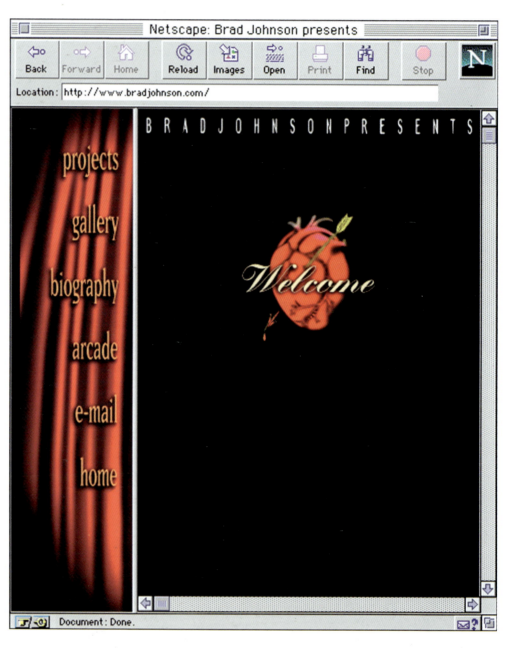

Communication Arts

Interactive Design Annual 1

Brad Johnson helped **Smetts Stafford Media** build the first ever Interactive Design Annual on CD ROM. The CD was sent to all subscribers in the September 1995 issue of **Communication Arts** and provides users with a unique opportunity to experience the best in interactive media. The CD is introduced with a Quicktime collage Brad composed with elements from the winning entries.

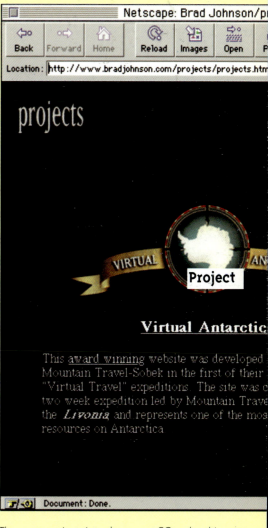

Netscape: Brad Johnson/p

Location: http://www.bradjohnson.com/projects/projects.htm

projects

Virtual Antarctic

This award winning website was developed Mountain Travel-Sobek in the first of their "Virtual Travel" expeditions. The site was o two week expedition led by Mountain Trave the *Livonia* and represents one of the mos resources on Antarctica

Document: Done.

The page, projects introduces past CG and multimedia designs. The CD-ROM is a collection of award-wining works from the *Communications Arts*. Brad Johnson has participated in the collage-making of QuickTime movie. (left)

Splash's Painting Gallery

The Old One-Piece

The Shoebox Shows

The Woods

Imagine Their Surprise!

Netscape: Brad Johnson presents

Back · Forward · Home · Reload · Images · Open · Print · Find · Stop

Location: http://www.bradjohnson.com/arcade/arcade.html

BRAD JOHNSON presents

pull here

Document: Done.

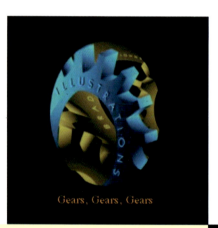

Gears, Gears, Gears

In Gallery, works with 3D illustrations of high quality are introduced. (Left)

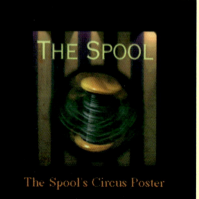

THE SPOOL

The Spool's Circus Poster

When you open the curtain according to the instruction in the section of arcade, you'll see the GIF animation of a cup of steaming coffee with the word "cream?" looking like it's been poured into it. And when you click "Wake up and smell the coffee?" or "No more coffee!" under the picture, you'll see humorous tricks. (left)

The Macromedia Director Movie called PINCH BRAND clothespins is the sales promotional movie for a imaginary brand of clothespins Pinch. It explains the materials and the functions of the product so seriously that it makes you laugh. In addition to this, the fantastic animated illustrations clearly show why this site has received many awards. (bottom)

www.dsiegel.com

DAVID SIEGEL

Welcome to my Casbah:David Siegel

(http://www.dsiegel.com)

This site is designed by David Siegel, who contributes to web design reviews "High Five". On the very first page, there is a collage in four different colors of pictures of Marilyn Monroe, reminding me of the artwork of Andy Warhol. It is accompanied by the words of the famous comedian, Lenny Bruce. There are four icons, each with a picture of Marilyn Monroe and each of which leads to menu pages. One menu page consists of nine images. The images are slightly different, but the contents are somewhat similar. The site offers his essays and journals, updated regularly, and the introduction of the sites produced by female designers. The site is full of enriching contents produced only by people who contributes to reviews of web design.

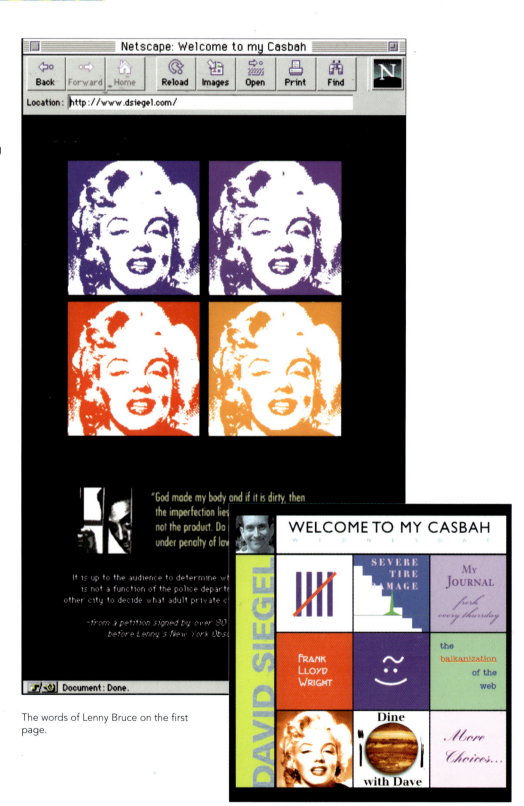

The words of Lenny Bruce on the first page.

David Siegel: Jack of None

Hi. I'm David Siegel. People call me a master of all trades and jack of none. Actually, nobody calls me that; I made it up. I was born in 1959 in Salt Lake City, Utah (is your cursor moving toward the "back" button yet?). Salt Lake has about 3,000 Jews. Now they're down to 2,998, because Roseanne Barr and I moved away. While both Roseanne and I have moved on to brighter pastures, most people manage not to confuse the two of us. Perhaps that's because she lives in Iowa and I live in Palo Alto.

I come from a totally functional family, a fact that surprises most of my friends. I spent most of my youth on and off the ski trails at places like Snowbird, Alta, and Park City. I have taught many people to ski and someday would like to make a killer video on teaching yourself to ski, because I believe the way ski schools do it is ridiculous. I can teach someone to ski the whole mountain in four days, from scratch, and I bristle every time I see them leading a row of ducks down the bunny hill. Perhaps I'll just have to open my own ski clinic right here.

I spent a year after high school in Israel on a kibbutz and in Jerusalem. Though I've forgotten how to speak Hebrew, it was one of the greatest experiences of my life. If you have time, go live on a kibbutz for six months before continuing to read on. It will make a big difference in your on-line phone bill. I also lived in Zermatt, Switzerland (imagine a hotlink that takes you there, and you explored it, and now you're back) where I met all kinds of great people and did not climb the Matterhorn.

I hitchhiked all around Europe with a baby-food jar of sourdough starter. Whoever gave me a ride I convinced to let me stay at his house and I would make him/her pancakes in the morning. In this way I cruised all over Switzerland having conversations with people in languages I did not speak. As a result, I fell in love with Swiss people and I still think (hope) that some day I will find a Swiss woman to, well, live happily ever after with. So if you are a nice Swiss girl looking for a green card, give me a call and we'll work something out. If you know any nice Swiss (or French or German) women, please tell them to come visit my web pages and send me a note. If you introduce me to my future wife, I'll make you the coolest web site you've ever seen, how's that?

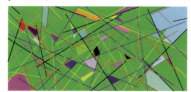

Okay, I lived in Boulder from 1978-1982 and didn't do any cocaine (if you knew Boulder back then, you'd appreciate this statement). I learned to rock climb and race road bikes and play with computers. I lived on Pearl Street, a block away from Dot's Diner and the Mall. I'd give anything for a hot-link that would take me from my house in Palo Alto back to Dot's Diner for their home-made buttermilk biscuits and german pancakes (whoops! I'm a vegan now, so I don't eat those things any more. Shoot!).

In 1982, I was asked by Donald Knuth to join the new Digital Typography department at Stanford, a cross between graphic design and computer science. I and my three grad-student counterparts, all of whom are now famous designers and type industry people, worked in the Metafont group figuring how to make typefaces that looked good come out of laser printers. There was Dan Mills, who is now manager of type production at Adobe Systems, Carol Twombly, who is now an internationally famous type designer whose typefaces, Lithos, Mirarae, Trajan, Charlemagne, Adobe Caslon, and others, grace everything from the New York Times to MTV. You literally cannot go a day in this country without seeing one of her typefaces. Cleo Huggins, also in our group, became famous for designing Sonata, Adobe's music font. We also had the pleasure of working with the amazing Scott Kim, whose "inversions" (letterforms and words that are symmetric in some way or other) are quite well known. Scott is now one of the country's leading game and puzzle designers. Wait til you see what he has in store for you next year.

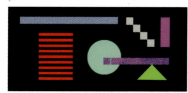

Our teachers were Donald Knuth and Charles Bigelow. Knuth, who bravely sponsored our work, is the world-famous author of the TEX typesetting language and a heck of a nice guy. Bigelow, one of the world's leading authorities on type, designed the famous Lucida series of typefaces with his studio partner, Kris Holmes. Together, they are two of the most talented and technically savvy type designers in the world today. In case you're getting bored, you may want to see a real photo of me that sits at the end of my casbah.

In working on my master's thesis, I had the good fortune of working with Hermann Zapf, the world-famous type designer who lives in Darmstadt, Germany. Zapf has designed dozens and dozens of typefaces, including Optima, Palatino, Zapf Chancery, Melior, and many others. Now, ten years later, he and I are collaborating on a new series of script typefaces that you will be able to buy in a year or so.

I got my master's degree and went to work at Lucasfilm, Ltd. In 1986, our computer group became Pixar. I got to work with many amazing people at Pixar, most of whom are now movers and shakers in the graphics industry. To name them all would simply be a who's-who of computer graphics pioneers. I loved being in a startup and having to do two hundred things at once, but eventually I knew I wasn't cut out to work for other people.

So, in January of 1987 (Gawd, if you went to be boring, tell everything, but if you really want to be boring, tell everything about yourself!!) I started painting computers. I had a booth at what might have been the third or fourth MacWorld Expo, and showed colored Macintoshes. Yes, I'm the guy who painted the Macs. I painted hundreds of Macintoshes in all kinds of colors and had a great time. Both at Pixar and in this painting business I learned how to not start a business.

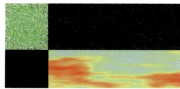

Then I designed a typeface called Tekton. Fred Brady at Adobe chose the name and gets a lot of credit for making Tekton into a real typeface. I thought architects might like it. I was wrong. Everyone liked it. For a while there, it was hard to get through a day without seeing it. Now that's not true. Now you see mostly ripoffs. They look like Tekton, but they are irregular, spindly, awkward, and ugly. At least they use the real Tekton in the McDonald's commercials.

I won't bore you with a rundown of my other typefaces. I lived in New York

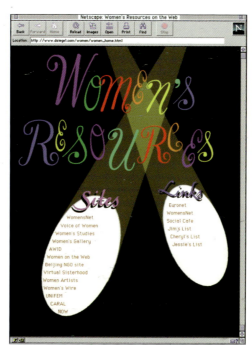

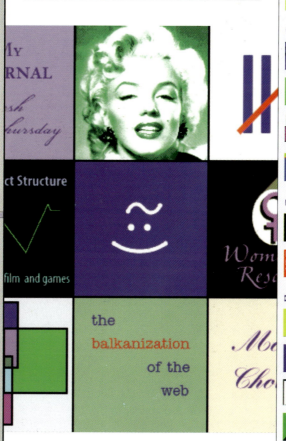

Please add this page to your hotlist and tell your friends to come visit! Tell them to enter through the casbah!

www.entropy8.com

Entropy 8

(http://www.entropy8.com)

While I was writing this book, this site was renewed, and the new one, was completely different from the old one. I decided to introduce the old one so as to preserve it, as it is truly fine. It is subtitled, " my labor of love and frustration", and so, because of the "my ", I imagine it is designed by one person. But, whether created by one person, several people or a large group of people, it is an incredible work. It is full of beautiful graphics, such as have never seen on Japanese sites, and full, too, of creative images and moving icons. This is one of the finest combinations of art and technology that I have seen.

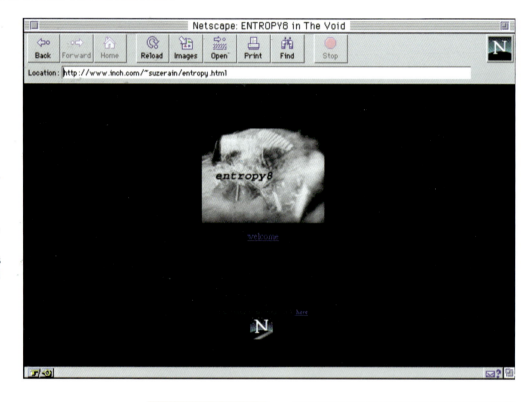

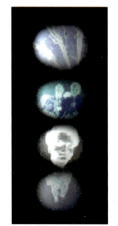

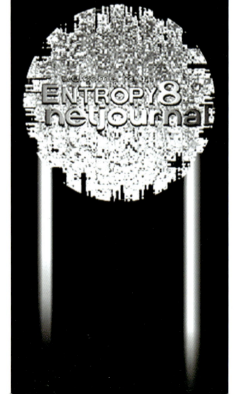

A movie of an exploding house on the first page. (upper right)
The designer's surrealistic art works. (bottom)

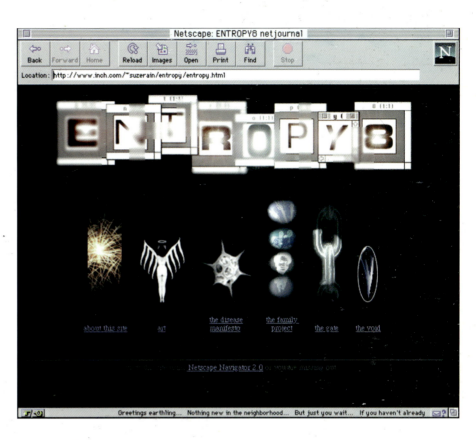

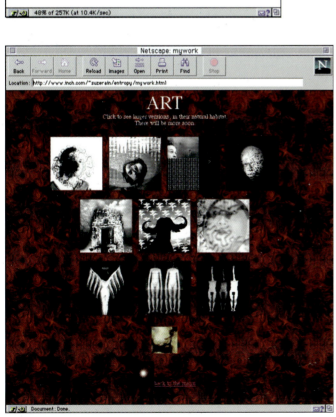

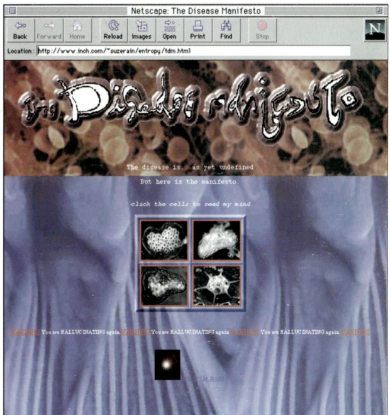

wings.buffalo.edu/~jcn

FACTOR DESIGN GROUP

(http://wings.buffalo.edu/~jcn)

Design/Product :Jason Napolitano

This site is located inside the server of the State University of New York (SUNY) at Buffalo. It is produced by Jason Napolitano, who is a SUNY student majoring in Communication Design. The site consists of his portfolio, an introduction of the links of the members of the Factor Design Group, (a group of students designers led by him), and an index of design institutes and other sites that he recommends. High-quality interface design is created with professional visual treatment.

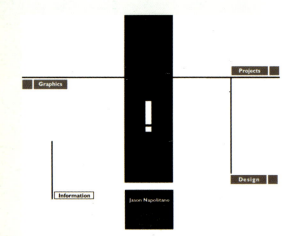

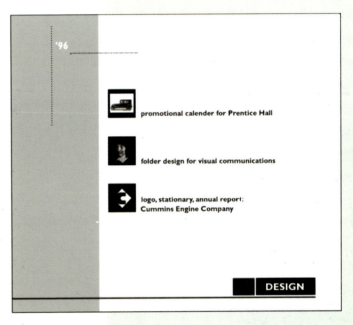

www.cibernet.it/thebox

thebox

the box

(http://www.cibernet.it/thebox)

Design/Product :Theo van Boxel
Copywriter : Maria Luisa Carrozza, Theo van Boxel
Programme : Theo van Boxel (shockwaves),
Claudio Montanari (server)

This is the site of Theo van Boxel, who lives in Pisa which is famous for Torre Pendente. I was impressed by his message expressing the substance of creation. His site reflects by his message, and it is chic and of good taste. It offers his portfolio of art works, a page of his advice for coloring, titled COLORE, an experimental page, information on Pisa, and a bookmark list. This is a typical individual site, on which the producer's interests are reflected. On the menu page, images marked by his strong individuality are laid out as the entrances of each sections. At a glance, the images do not seem to be connected with the themes of the sections; however, by observing the images closely, I feel I can understand his mind. It is still something of a problem, though, and it may be because of the malfunction of the network circuit that I could not download 1.3 MB data of his portfolio. I would like to see the contents of the section whose icon is a cave painting of a cow at Altamira.

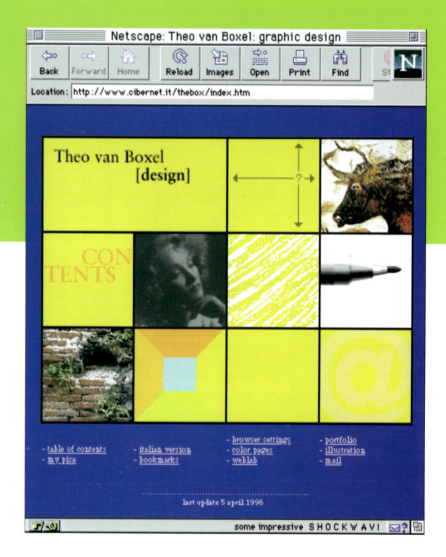

the 0 . computer design

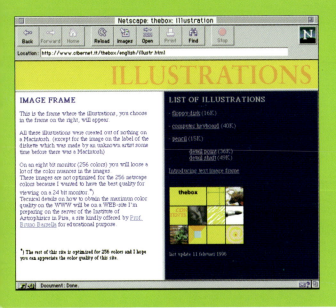

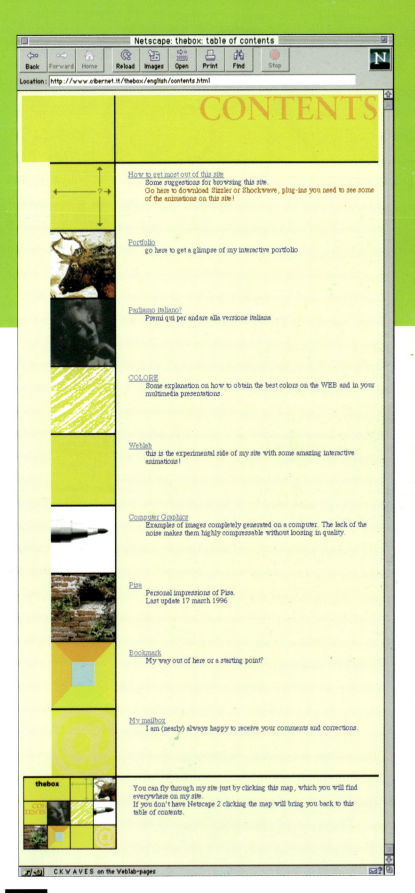

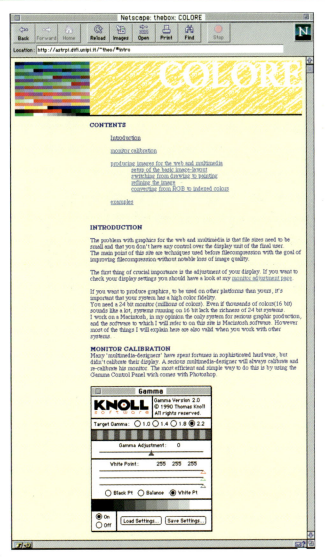

www.wnn.or.jp/wnn-x

The Microscopic Structured Garden of Kenji Kohiyama

(http://www.wnn.or.jp/wnn-x)

Production : NTT (Nippon Telegraph and Telephone Corporation), NTT Learning Systems Corporation, Kaitaishinsha
Content : Kenji Kohiyama (NTT / NTT Advanced Technology Corporation)
Planner : Tetuo Fukaya (Kaitaishinsha)
Art Director : Eisuke Maita (NTT Learning Systems Corporation)
Creative Director : Shinji Kojima (NTT Learning Systems Corporation)
Copywriter : Emiko Yokokawa (Kaitaishinsha)
Designer : Koji Kono
HTML Writer : Miyuki Sudo (NTT Learning Systems Corporation)
Programmer : Nobuyuki Mochizuki (NTT Learning Systems Corporation)

This is the site which is operated by NTT, a Japan's representative multimedia networking company. As a result, it is high quality and full of information. It is divided into three sections, The Labyrinth to Poetic Sentiment, The Labyrinth to Multi-focus and The Labyrinth to Tiling, where the author's collection of weevils and butterflies are beautifully displayed. Regarding the visual images, the details are well designed; for example, enlarged pictures of the weevils are displayed in a "sketch-book", whose pages you can turn. These elaborate designs are remarkably different from the individual sites of typical insect maniacs. And the site is also full of texts worth reading. The pictures of butterflies are presented with information on the places, dates and times of the photographing. In The Labyrinth to Tiling and on the page of the collection of weevils, the designing processes are carefully presented. I feel these details can be only provided by professionals, such as Kohiyama, an NTT engineer who helped design this site.

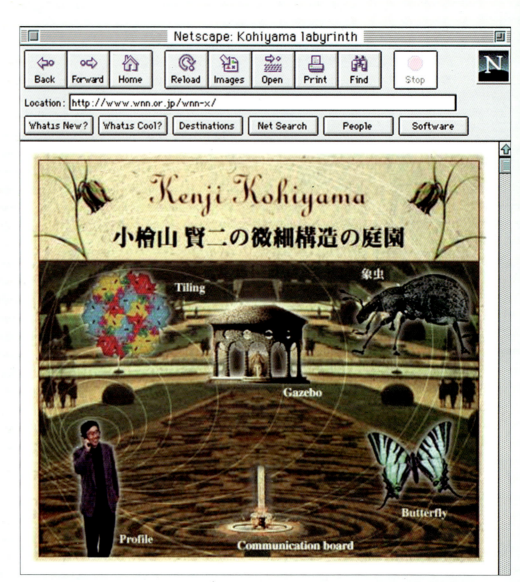

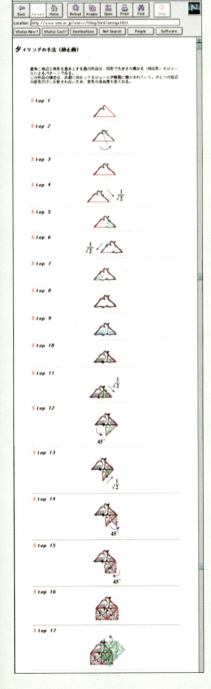

Examples of tiling and instructions for their design. (left & right)
Pictures of weevils. (bottom)

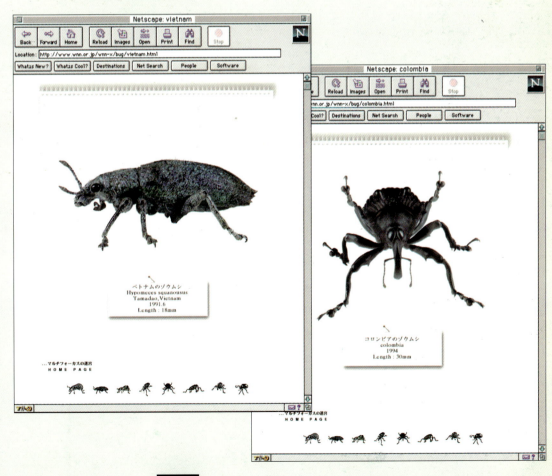

neog.com/wean/ weandesign.html

Mike Wean's Portfolio

(http://neog.com/wean/weandesign.html)

Mike Wean can be called a genius of graphic art design. He specializes in designing posters and books, and also writing comic books. The site offers his biography and art works, and the introduction of links he recommends. The section of his art works is really well worth seeing.

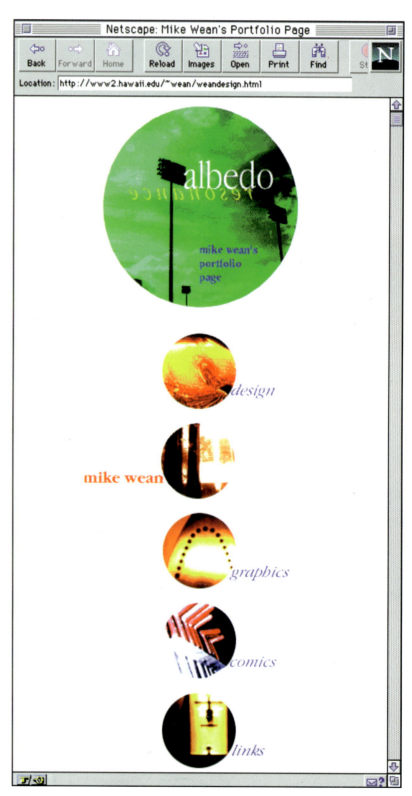

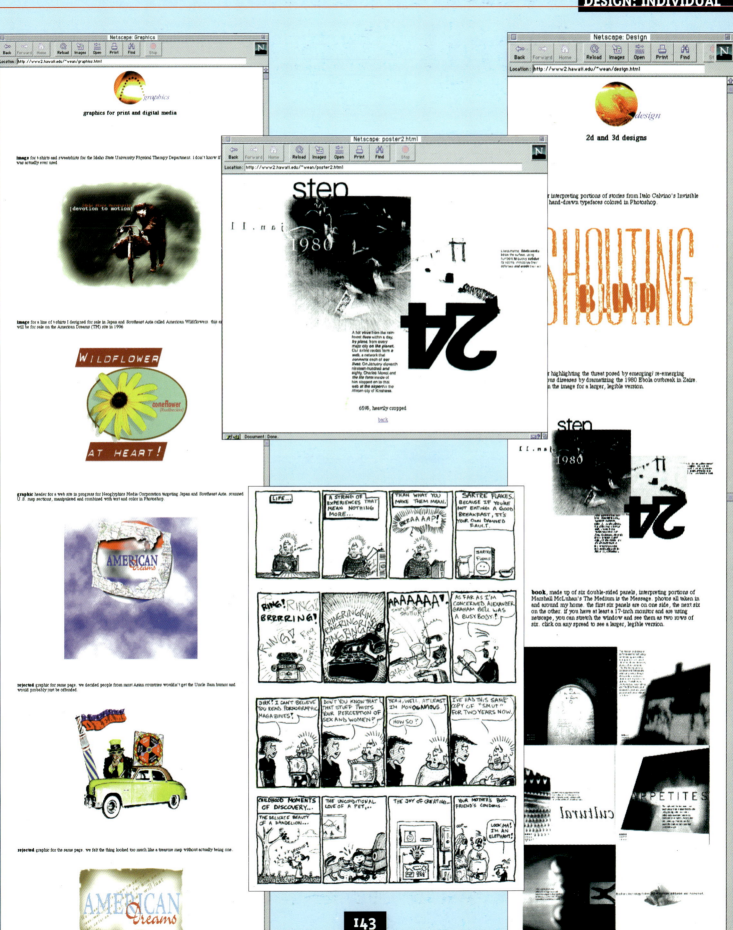

www.icmall.com/ce/ elena.html

Elena Design

(http://www.icmall.com/ce/elena.html)

Design/Production Firm : Elena Design
Art Director/Design : Elena Baca
Copywriter : Elena Baca
HTML Writer : Cody Wilson

This site is the personal portfolio of Élena Baca, a freelance designer living in Texas. She specializes in designing logos, print media as well as web sites. The colors of the whole images are chic, and the simple layout presents her art works very well. The designs of icons and heading images are feminine and sophisticated.

Elena Baca

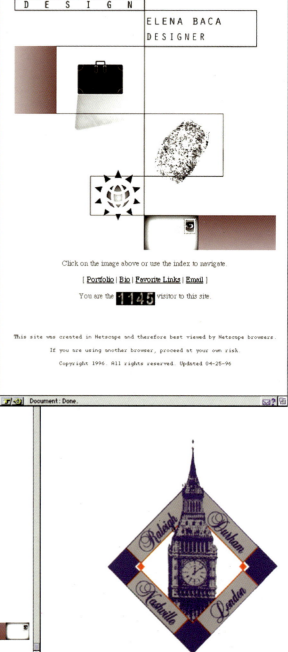

www.aloha.net/ ~perrine

Cyber Reef

(http://www.aloha.net/~perrine)

Design/Product : Ralph Perrine

The site is designed by Ralph Perrine, a graphic designer and illustrator living in Hawaii and it offers a mixture of his high-quality art works and an introduction to his choice of sites. Especially, the list of the sites he recommends is interesting.

users.aimnet.com/ ~bgakca

Brent Alexander | portfolio

Brent Alexander Portfolio

(http://users.aimnet.com/~bgakca)

Design/Production Firm : Dominik Malaise
Design : Brent Alexander

The black tool bar on a white background is impressive. The site is divided into four sections: graphics, interface, testsite and resume. The site shows some art works of Brent Alexander.

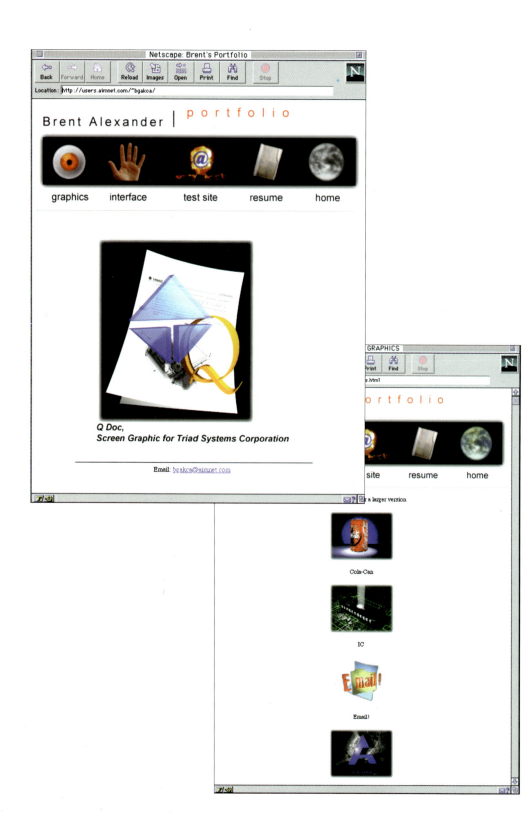

andro.sfc.keio. ac.jp/eto

Welcome to Eto's Possible World!

(http://andro.sfc.keio.ac.jp/eto)

Design/Product : Eto Kouichiro

This is the personal homepage of a student of SFC, Keio University. The typography of his name, simple icons and pastel colors of the texts give a fresh image. The layouts of the graphics and texts and the usage of the table tags are good examples.

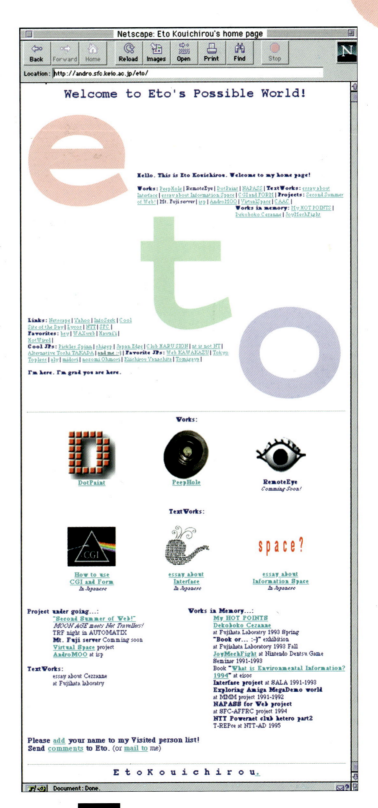

204.97.127.32/
JDK_Home.html

Jager Di Paola Kemp Design

(http://204.97.127.32/JDK_Home.html)

Design/Product : Jager Di Paola Kemp Design

The graphic images and the phrases on this site (exquisite corpse and the Consciousness of Chaos) seem to give us some philosophical messages. This is the site of a design team. To control the layout carefully, the texts are also treated as graphic files. The site includes a beautiful portfolio page, but the grotesque illustrations, for example, the image of a skull with its brains and eyes dropping out, have a somewhat negative impact. I would rather like to see more art works with an emphasis on design. The company's clients are Converse, TDK, a leather manufacturer, Coach, etc., for whom they provide various services including building brand identities, designing products, merchandising, producing videos and interactive media.

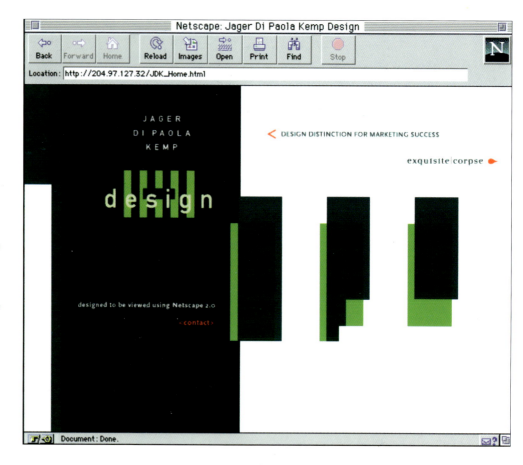

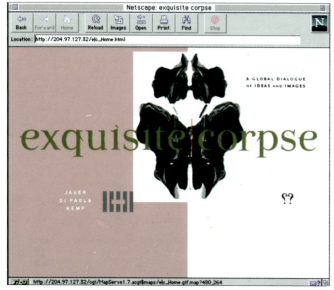

www.users.interport.
net/~ trinity

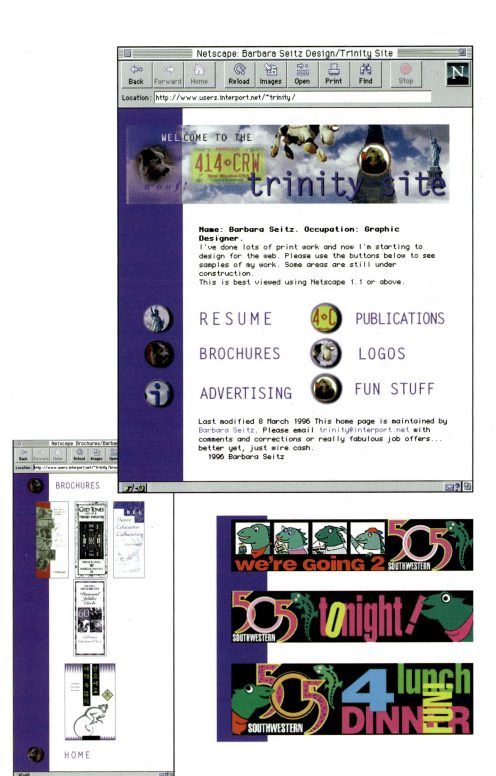

Barbara Seitz Design

(http://www.users.interport.net/~trinity)

Design/Production Firm : Barbara Seitz Design
Design : Barbara Seitz

This site is designed to promote her own art works. She says that she feels this site is the place to train herself for designing other web sites. She does not use any gimmicks like Server Push or GIF animation, but the color combination of her typography, the icons and the heading collage tell of her experience as a designer for print media.

www.3dsite.com/cgi/ resumes/don_st_mars/dsm.html

Don St. Mars

(http://www.3dsite.com/cgi/resumes/ don_st_mars/dsm.html)

This is the personal site of a graphic designer, Don St. Mars, who works for Nickelodeon, an American cable TV for children. The colors, typography and layout are simple and sophisticated. There are as well some humorous expressions, such as the winding pencil 3D image on the first page.

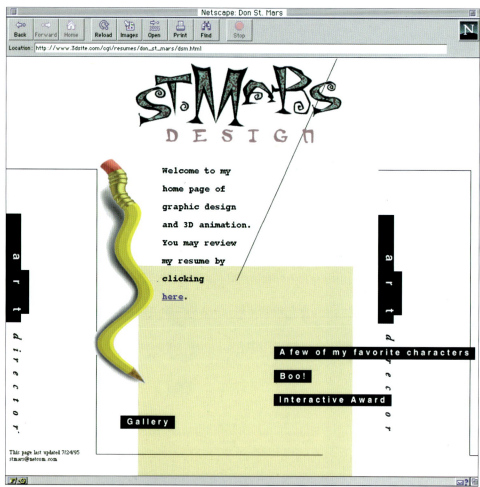

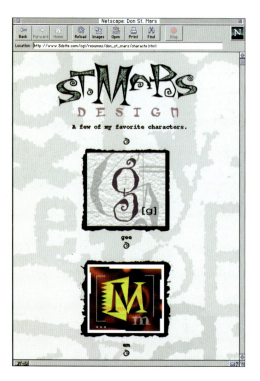

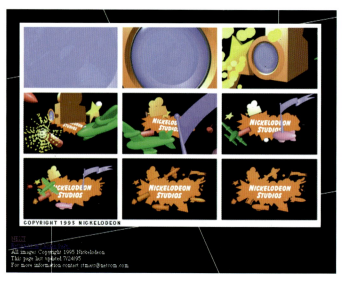

www.fns.net/~mrosica

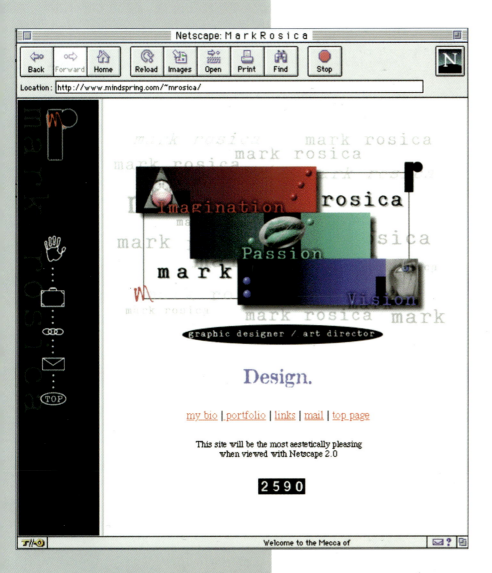

Mark Rosica Designs

(http://www.fns.net/~mrosica)

Design/Production Firm : Mark Rosica Designs
Design : Mark Rosica

This is the site produced by an individual designer and it gives various possibilities of icons, typography and coloring. It is too bad that the sections are not yet completed. I look forward to seeing it when it is done.

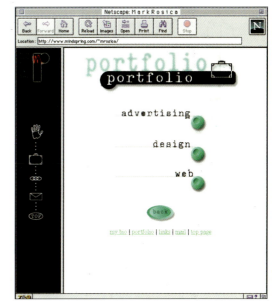

www.dag.nl/ 1000%max

1000% Max

(http://www.dag.nl/1000%max)

Design/Production Firm : 1000%MAX
Client :1000%MAX
Art Director : Peter van den Hoogen
Designer : Peter van den Hoogen
Illustrator : Peter van den Hoogen
Photographer : Oski Colado
HTML Writer : Peter van den Hoogen
Programmer : Vincent Hillenbrink
Others :
Lara Ankersmit (Thinktank)
Martin Terpstra (Technical Support)
Ben Hendriks (Quicktime Movie)

This site is a cybersonic web magazine compiled by two youths in the Netherlands. Well designed pop art graphics and illustrations will stimulate users' interests. When I accessed the site, it happened to have a special feature on a Japanese female duet band, Cibo Matto. Users can make links to categories such as Archive, Bands, Sensor, and Profile by clicking each menu in a column on the left side. While most of the information is available in English, a few reports are only in Dutch, which results in creating an exotic image.

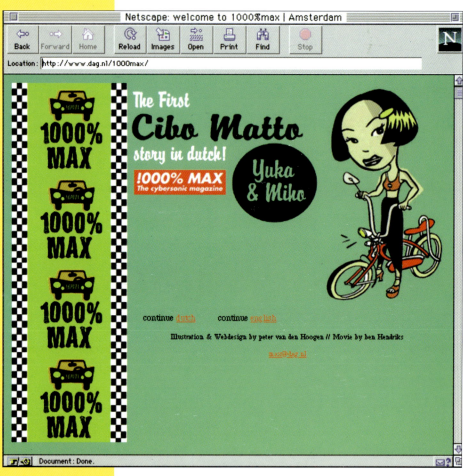

austinhealey.com

Big Healeys

(http://austinhealey.com)

Design/Production Firm : Roger Los Design
Design : Roger Los

This page is dedicated to enthusiasts for Austin Healey, once a popular light-weight sports car. The site provides a variety of information on Healey. It was designed by Roger Los, who must be one of the enthusiasts, but also includes comments from other Healey owners. It is designed with a frame function as a base and can be navigated to other sections by clicking frames at the top and bottom of the screen. Visitors will find a "Healey catalog" particularly interesting. They can illustrate a car on a screen just by selecting desired colors of mini-icons arranged vertically on the right side of the screen. Although the technique used in this site is simple, it is a good guide to use to make a catalog with a frame function.

factory colors

■ = interior

choose any of the interiors for each color

black

florida green

british racing green

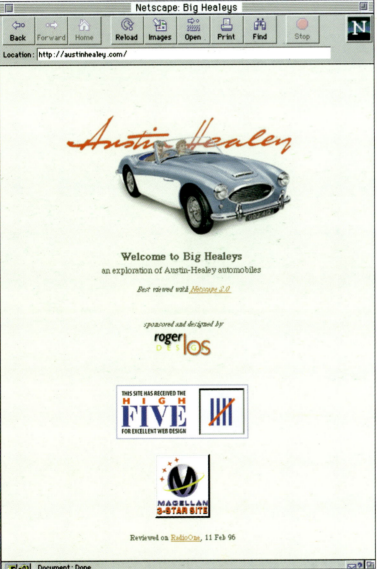

www.zonezero.com

ZONEZERO

(http://www.zonezero.com)

Design/Production Firm : Pedro Meyer
Design : Pedro Meyer
HTML Writer : Pedro Meyer, Jonathan Reff

This art gallery site is led by Pedro Mayer, who created a sensational multimedia title "I Photograph to Remember" at the time of the launch of CD-ROMs. It presents works of more than 20 photographers along with excellent essays. Meyer's intention, "to have a work talk for itself" has, made its design as a whole simple and sincere. Viewers can also find a page to check the calibration of the monitor. We can see the importance attached to visuality in this site.

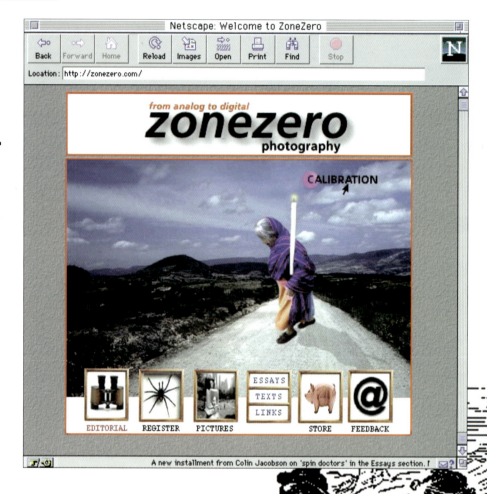

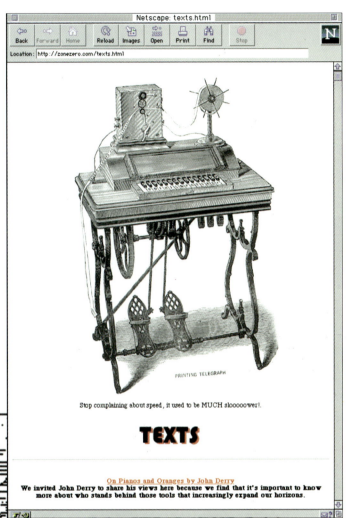

Netscape: texts.html

Back Forward Home Reload Images Open Print Find Stop

Location: http://zonezero.com/texts.html

PRINTING TELEGRAPH

Stop complaining about speed, it used to be MUCH slooooower!.

TEXTS

On Pianos and Oranges by John Derry

We invited John Derry to share his views here because we find that it's important to know more about who stands behind those tools that increasingly expand our horizons.

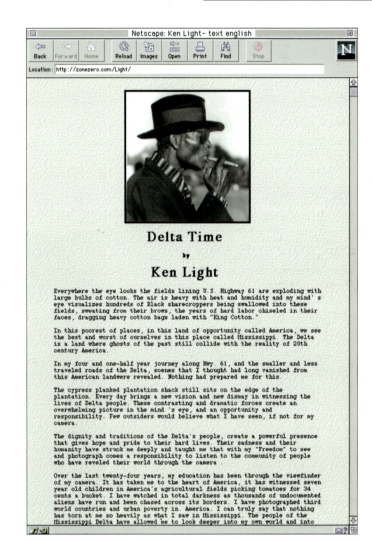

Netscape: Ken Light- text english

Back Forward Home Reload Images Open Print Find Stop

Location: http://zonezero.com/Light/

Delta Time

by

Ken Light

Everywhere the eye looks the fields lining U.S. Highway 61 are exploding with large bulbs of cotton. The air is heavy with heat and humidity and my mind's eye visualizes hundreds of Black sharecroppers being swallowed into these fields, sweating from their brows, the years of hard labor chiseled in their faces, dragging heavy cotton bags laden with "King Cotton."

In this poorest of places, in this land of opportunity called America, we see the best and worst of ourselves in this place called Mississippi. The Delta is a land where ghosts of the past still collide with the reality of 20th century America.

In my four and one-half year journey along Hwy. 61, and the smaller and less traveled roads of the Delta, scenes that I thought had long vanished from this American landwere revealed. Nothing had prepared me for this.

The cypress planked plantation shack still sits on the edge of the plantation. Every day brings a new vision and new dismay in witnessing the lives of Delta people. These contrasting and dramatic forces create an overwhelming picture in the mind's eye, and an opportunity and responsibility. Few outsiders would believe what I have seen, if not for my camera.

The dignity and traditions of the Delta's people, create a powerful presence that gives hope and pride to their hard lives. Their sadness and their humanity have struck me deeply and taught me that with my "Freedom" to see and photograph comes a responsibility to listen to the community of people who have reveled their world through the camera.

Over the last twenty-four years, my education has been through the viewfinder of my camera. It has taken me to the heart of America, it has witnessed seven year old children in America's agricultural fields picking tomatoes for 34 cents a bucket. I have watched in total darkness as thousands of undocumented aliens have run and been chased across its borders. I have photographed third world countries and urban poverty in America. I can truly say that nothing has torn at me so heavily as what I saw in Mississippi. The people of the Mississippi Delta have allowed me to look deeper into my own world and into

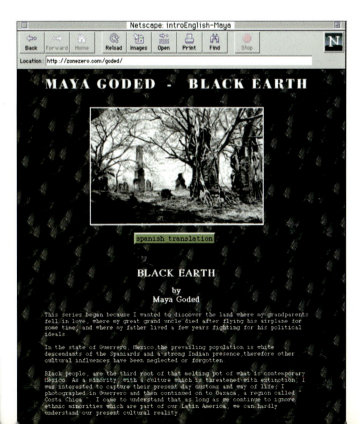

Netscape: introEnglish-Maya

Back Forward Home Reload Images Open Print Find Stop

Location: http://zonezero.com/goded/

MAYA GODED - BLACK EARTH

spanish translation

BLACK EARTH

by

Maya Goded

This series began because I wanted to discover the land where my grandparents fell in love, where my great grand uncle died after flying his airplane for some time, and where my father lived a few years fighting for his political ideals.

In the state of Guerrero, Mexico,the prevailing population is white descendants of the Spaniards and a strong Indian presence,therefore other cultural influences have been neglected or forgotten.

Black people, are the third root of that melting pot of what is contemporary Mexico. As a minority, with a culture which is threatened with extinction, I was interested to capture their present day customs and way of life; I photographed in Guerrero and then continued on to Oaxaca, a region called Costa Chica. I came to understand that as long as we continue to ignore ethnic minorities which are part of our Latin America, we can hardly understand our present cultural reality.

www.cyber24.com

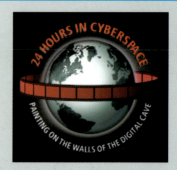

24 Hours In Cyberspace

(http://www.cyber24.com)

24 Hours In Cyberspace was started by
Rick Smolan, who produced From Alcie
To Ocean, a well-known CD-ROM
masterpiece. Attempting to create a
digital time capsule, this site has a
collection of more than 200,000
photographs, which were shot by
hundreds of photojournalists on
February 8, 1996. Visitors can always
enjoy updated information with high-
quality photographs along with
supplementary stories. It is not too much
to say that this well-prepared and
elaborate design makes this site one of
the best in the area of web journalism.

Image of film surrounding the earth on the front
page. It indicates that a myriad number of different
lives are led all over the world every day. To
interpret this from the view point of movie makers,
film is moving round the earth, which is rotating in
the opposite direction.

Netscape: A Digital Time Capsule

Back | Forward | Home | Reload | Images | Open | Print | Find | Stop

Location: http://www.cyber24.com/

ENTER HERE

THE GOAL WAS TO CREATE A DIGITAL TIME CAPSULE OF HOW
ONLINE TECHNOLOGY IS CHANGING THE WORLD
IN THE COURSE OF A SINGLE DAY

You are about to enter a digital time capsule, an
extraordinary collection of photographs taken on a
single, ordinary day - Thursday, February 8, 1996.
These images, captured by 1,000 professional and
amateur photographers dispatched to every
continent, record how the online world is changing
our lives. No picture here is more then 24 hours
older or younger than any other. And every
photograph was shot for a single purpose: to
document the harmonies and paradoxes of life in
cyberspace as it was lived on this one day.

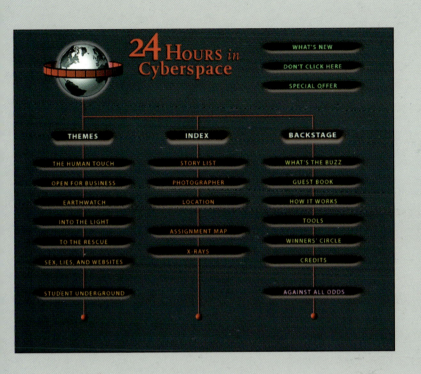

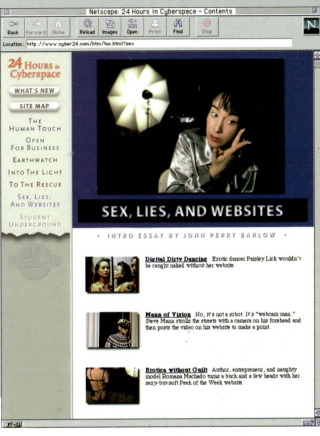

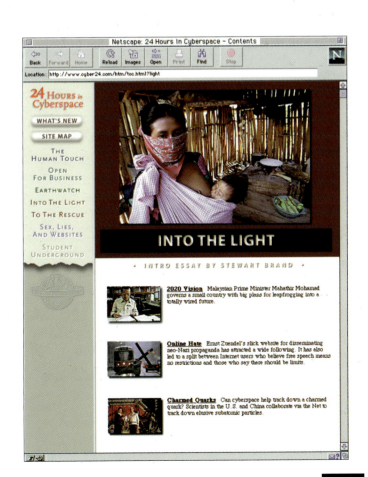

www.artnetweb.com

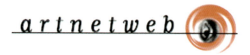

artnetweb

(http://www.artnetweb.com)

This on-line exhibition takes full advantage of characteristics of the WWW. As this page hosts an exhaustive collection of links to other sites on the net, visitors easily forget which site they started from as they access different sites and enjoy art works one after another. There are many homepages that have links to other related sites, but this artnetweb is one of the few where visitors become unconcerned about the location of particular sites. Properly speaking, it is important for visitors to access the Internet, not a particular web site. This attempt clarifies the characteristics of the Web. At the same time, by commonly using the limited resources, it has proved the true worth of Internet.

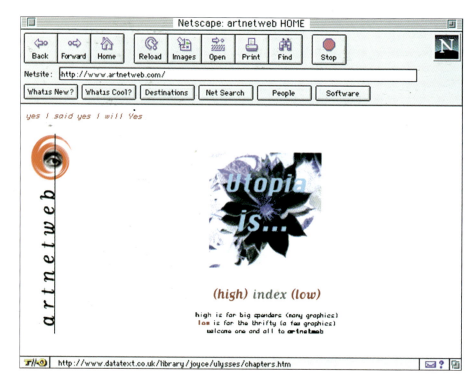

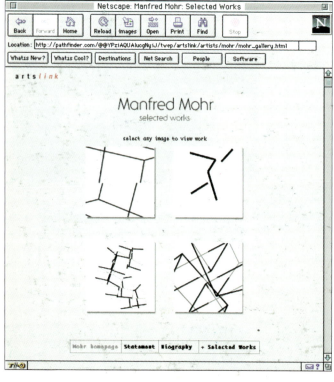

Linking icon to access The Speared Peanut Award, which also leads to other various art scenes.

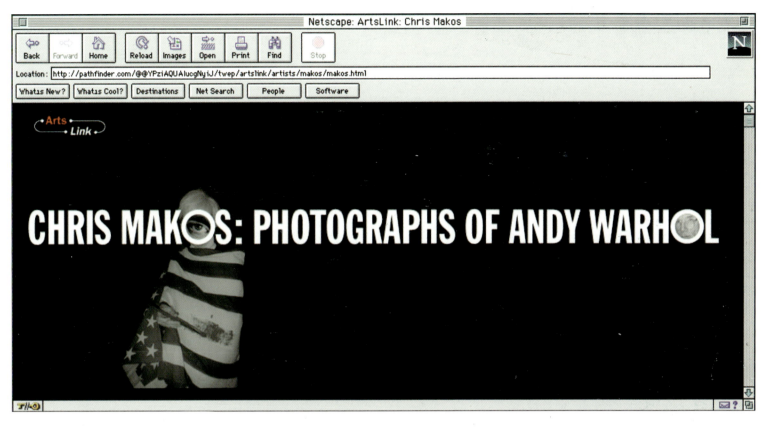

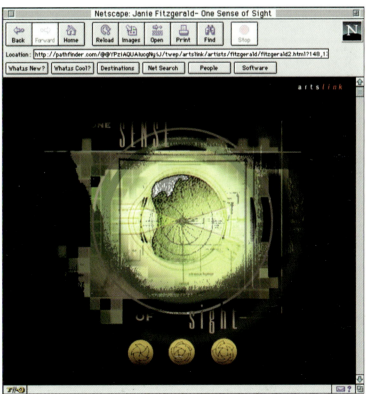

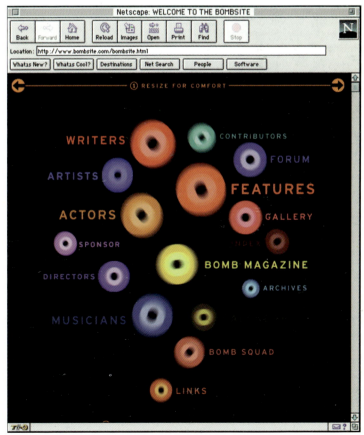

Page displaying art works of a linked site. The works in artslink page in the Time Warner Pathfinder are frequently accessed by visitors. By the way, does a black background always happen to be used on well-designed pages?

www.istorm.com/ burningman

Burning Man

(http://www.istorm.com/burningman)

Design/Production Firm : i-STORM Studios
Client :The Burning Man Project
Art Director : David Beach
Creative Director : David Beach
Copywriter : Stuart Mangrum
Designer : Cale Peeples
Illustrator : Cale Peeples
Photographer : Various
HTML Writer : Erik Salmonson
Programmer : Erik Salmonson
Others : Dan Vendrell

I was impressed with the metaphor of its design. When I first accessed its front page to find a picture of a large-sized notebook on parched and cracked ground, I could not imagine what would come next. After clicking it, a picture of the notebook overspreading the screen turned up. This layout is skillfully created by making use of a frame function (of Netscape expansion) in a way I had never seen before. Viewers will discover how well and carefully it is prepared. For instance, an image of a bookmark of the notebook page is designed to become a clickable map which leads to other information. It is also noteworthy that the four corners of the pictures are pasted with tapes as if they were real. The quality of its icon images and photographs cannot be overlooked, either. I had no idea what Burning Man was until access to this page. Burning Man is an annual festival held in a desert in Northern Nevada, where thousands of artists, performers and free spirits converge at the end of summer. The name of the festival was derived from the ritual burning of an enormous human effigy. Photographs of the ritual are also provided in this site.
As many homepages besides this site cover this festival, the event must be a very popular in the United States. On-line Media such as HotWired, DiscoveryOnline, and CNN have reports on this event.

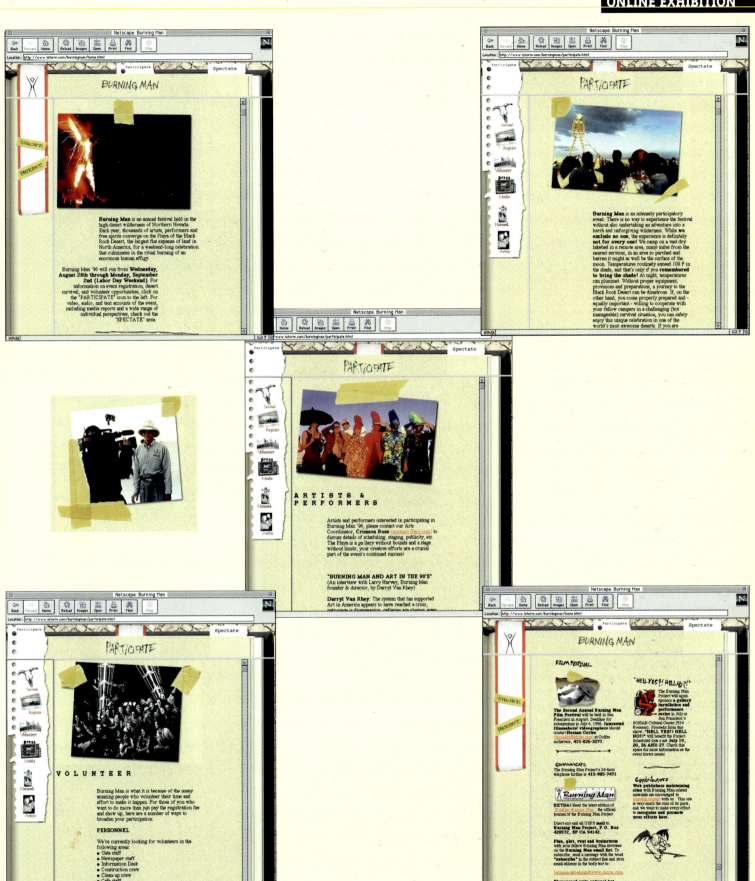

www.oracle.co.jp

Oracle Corporation Japan

(http://www.oracle.co.jp)

Client : Oracle Corporation Japan
Production : Kinotrope, Inc.
Art Director : Masahiro Ikuta
Director : Kazuya Ouchi
Designer : Kazuhiro Hayase,Honami Morita
Illustrator : Misako Aono, Kazuo Miwa
HTML Writer : Kenjiro Makino
Programmer : Toshimi Aoki
Agency : Aspec, Inc.

This site starts with a variety of seasonal large-sized pictures as the main graphic. The pictures harmonize with icon images and background colors accordingly. On a page of moon and carp, for example, the waxing and waning of the moon and the color of the carp change in various ways whenever the server side processes programming. Another example is on a page of butterflies and lotus flowers, where the illustrations, icons, and background change in three ways- morning, daytime, and night versions- depending upon what time users have access the site. It is difficult to develop a homepage in a Japanese text environment because of its font, of which types and sizes are controlled by the client side of a web site. The Oracle homepage, however, successfully avoided this problem by reducing the use of text to the minimum and marking most of the graphic data instead. Layouts are carefully prepared with intricate arrangement of table tags to make every browser screen look well- balanced. Although graphics of the WWW in other countries besides Japan are inclined to demonstrate too much computer-aided techniques like "high- tech" and "3-D", there should be other ways to design high-quality imagery. Impressions of homepages largely relies on its graphic image irrespective of its "digitalness". This homepage was in fact produced by a content provider team that I belong to. We have the confidence that this project is a milestone that has directed us to where we are now.

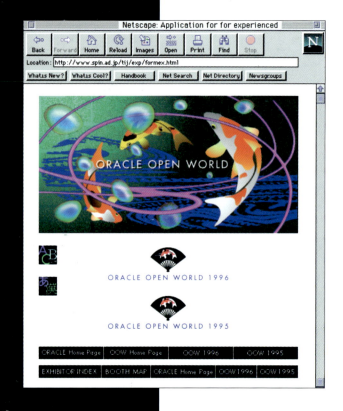

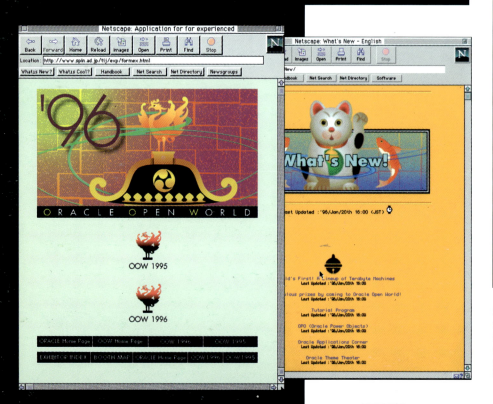

Homepage to provide information on events by which Oracle Corporation Japan takes the lead within Oracle Group. It is intended to provide information not only to domestic users but also to a worldwide audience. A wide range of ideas and devices give it a festive mood.

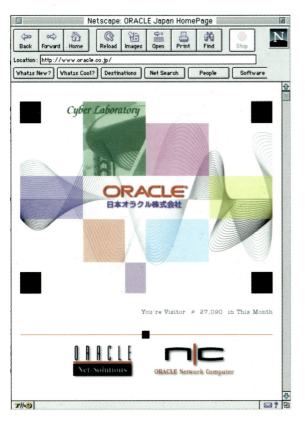

Cyber Laboratory

ORACLE
日本オラクル株式会社

You're Visitor # 27,090 in This Month

ORACLE Net-Solutions

n|c
ORACLE Network Computer

The Net is a design concept of this new homepage which was revised in July 1996. An interactive menu in Java language is presented on a cover page. (left)
The Products Encyclopedia page is dedicated to information on Oracle products. (right)
The Press Center page always offers most up-to-date news. (left, bottom)

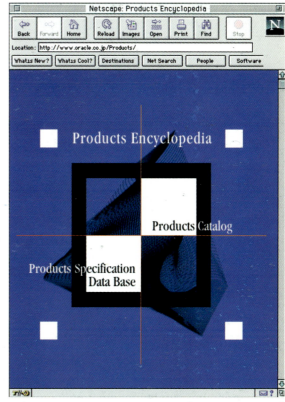

Products Encyclopedia

Products Catalog

Products Specification Data Base

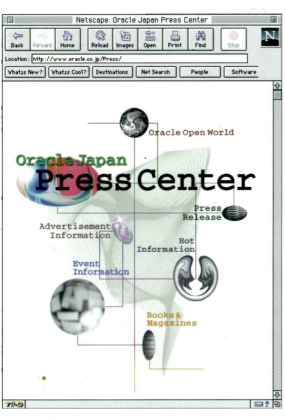

Oracle Open World

Oracle Japan
Press Center

Press Release

Advertisement Information

Hot Information

Event Information

Books & Magazines

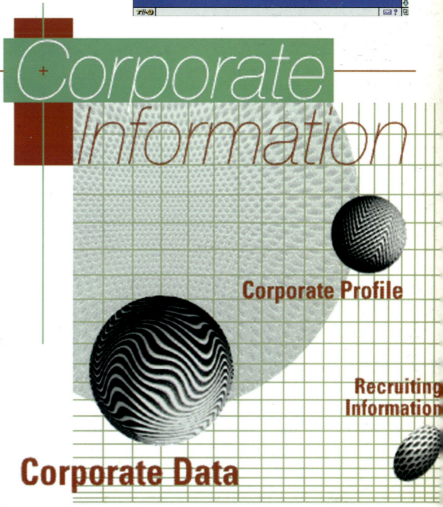

Corporate Information

Corporate Profile

Recruiting Information

Corporate Data

www.idsoftware.com

id Software

(http://www.idsoftware.com)

This is the homepage for id Software, the well-known provider of the popular network game "Doom". It is designed to convey an occult mood by displaying motifs associated with voodoo (the heathens) and keeping the use of text to the minimum. Texts are thoroughly controlled by using fonts in the shape of a cross and then filing them as a graphic file. It is unbelievable how the author was able to create the ideas and expressions in this graphic image. The content of the site itself is for practical use, as is known to the fans of their games, and links to a trial version of each game are available for downloading.

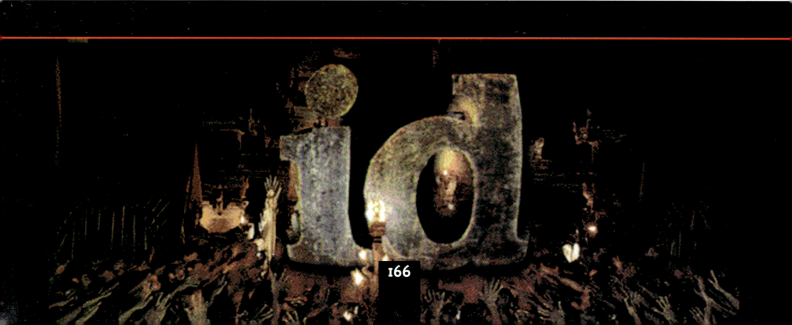

Several kinds of goods presented to an altar of the god of id (index page).
People worshipping the god of id (below on previous page).
Both have horror-stricken voodoo images.

KILLER GAMES

ULTIMATE DOOM

DOOM II

FINAL DOOM

HERETIC: SHADOW OF THE SERPENT RIDERS

HEXEN

VINTAGE ID

QUAKE

Heretic | Doom II | Hexen | Ultimate Doom | Quake | Vintage Games

The Main Page | Death Match Maker | Shopping Maul | Archives

id | Hot New Stuff | Killer Games | Friends of id

© 1996 Id Software, Inc. All Rights Reserved.

A crowd of skeletons screaming. What a messy place I have entered...This page presents their game software products. (above)
This font type is a perfect match for the design of its homepage. (next page, top left)

Available in June

Quake Update | Latest Info | Hot New Items

RELEASES

S   S

chnology Solutions PR

pings has networking

nd customizable keys to be
be the Macintosh. Enhanced

or the First Time, id Will
n to Contain Full Version

only anticipated computer.

id Bios | Press Releases

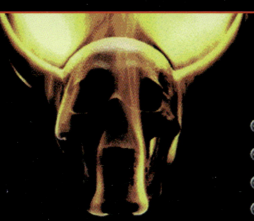

HOT
STUFF

⊛ QUAKE UPDATE
⊛ LATEST INFO
⊛ HOT NEW ITEMS
⊛ MAIN

www.voyagerco.com

VOYAGER

Voyager

(http://www.voyagerco.com)

This site is created by
Patty ABT, Sean Anderson, Francine Douwes,
Peter Flynn, Peter Girardi, Paul Klinger, John Porter,
Paul Schrynemakers, Reid Sherline,
Andy Stevens, and Andrew Zipern,
Editing : Dave Ekrem
Graphic Production : Fernando Music
Audio Production : Rex Arthur, Michael Wiese
The Criterion Collection :
Catherine Gray, Peter Becker,
Gordon Reynolds, Mary G. Pratt,
Nancy Bauer, Katrina Bauer
Voyager CDLink : Steve Riggins
Grand Street : Joshua Mack
The Green Room : Lisa Pedicini
The Guerrilla Girls : Rebecca Katz, Nicole Phelps
Digital Video : Peter Becker, J. J. Gifford
Programming : Alejandro Heyworth
Webmaster : Andrew Stevens, Ph. D.

This site is a homepage for Voyager Corporation, which pioneered CD/FD based multi-media by producing "Expanded Book". As they originally started their business by designing titles for laser disk films, the site covers a substantial collection of their own taste, ranging from movies, music CDs, and graphic novels, to font shops and projects by popular artists. Frequent updating has resulted in such a huge amount of information that we can hardly browse all of them. Its design is also developed elaborately, which is quite obvious icon and typographies on the front page. Background images are also revised occasionally. Furthermore, graphic images and text layouts on the document source page, are carefully designed by making the best use of tags of various levels and then cutting and pasting graphics to match each tag. In fact, opening and studying document sources whenever you find an interesting graphic images which draws your interest is the best way of practicing design layout with HTML. As a whole, that this site was produced by professionals who are fully aware that a high-quality of packaging is indispensable to have users appreciate the quality of content. This site has already implemented the on-line distribution of information on a large scale. They sell products such as above-mentioned fonts and a title of "Expanded Book".

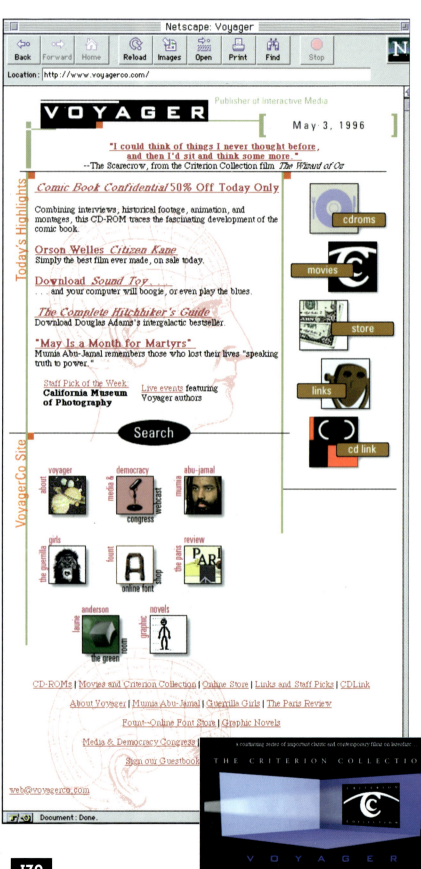

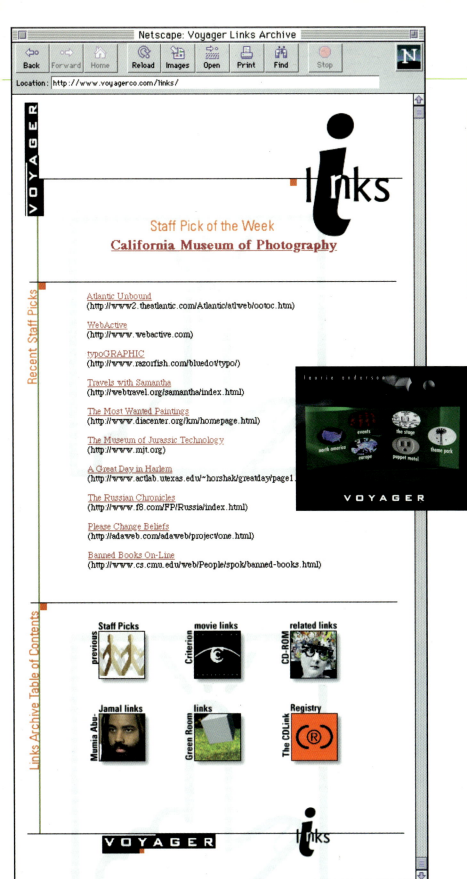

A new type of multi-media is experienced here on "CDlink" page, where existing music CD and WWW are combined with its own technological device.

www.agfa.com

AGFA

(http://www.agfa.com)

From this homepage, I learned that AGFA, originally a filmmaker, has laid considerable stress on the area of computer image processing upon being influenced by the recent trends of digitalization. Its layout is relatively simple with user friendliness given as top priority, but the good-quality header graphics show the sense of a company that is also sensitive to presentation. In conjunction with their principal business, this site also includes a section which offers a number of beautiful photographs where viewers can enjoy turning pages to their hearts' content.

Imaging Solutions

Netscape: Nauset Beach

Back | Forward | Home | Reload | Images | Open | Print | Find | Stop

Location: http://www.agfahome.com/features/dezitter/nauset.html

DIGITAL DE ZITTER

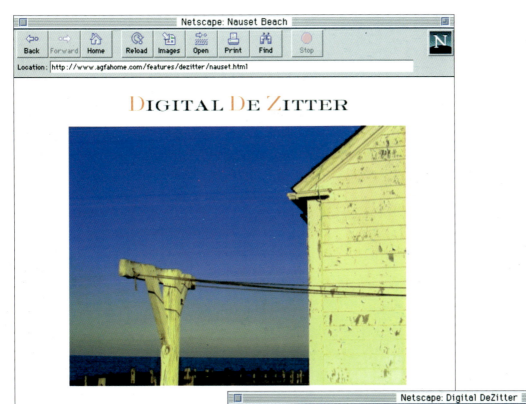

"I said to my wife Erica, let's take Nelson and
at the Nauset Coast Guard station. It was a late
sunlight left, hitting this weathered old Cape b
one-rail fence, and the ocean -- it's just so clas
and bump up the blues and play with the golds

ut AGFA

Harry's t

• Message from the Ch
• Historical Highlights
• Agfa Organisation
• Agfa Worldwide

Netscape: Digital DeZitter

Back | Forward | Home | Reload | Images | Open | Print | Find | Stop

Location: http://www.agfahome.com/features/dezitter/home.html

DIGITAL DE ZITTER
(CLICK IMAGE FOR ENLARGED VIEW)

Sidewalk/SF

Winter Sky

Interior/SF

Turnstiles

Nelson Running

Nauset Beach

Mailbox Detail

Flowers #2

Brewster #1

Stage Harbor #1

Still Life #2 SF

Still Life/SF

Street Light/NYC

Pier #1/
Stage Harbor

Pier #2/
Stage Harbor

salsa.walldata.com

Club SALSA

(http://salsa.walldata.com)

Design/Production Firm : Dave McKean
Client : Wall Data Incorporated
Art Director : Dave McKean
Creative Director : Dave McKean
Copywriter : Dave McKean
Designer : Dave McKean
Illustrator : Dave McKean

This web site was produced by a graphic artist Dave McKean at a request of the software company Wall Data Incorporated. It is a complete first-class homepage without any indication of complicated high-tech. A story at the Latin Club is developed as a metaphor to provide information on the client's products. Topics are categorized in the form of club rooms, such as Center Stage, Havana Lounge, La Clavé Bar, Boss' Office, and Alonzo's Attic. It provides serial stories to encourage users' repeated visit. There is also a service available to send an e-mail message to users whenever a new episode of the serial is created. McKean is a graphic artist who published a number of books and CD-ROMs. He also writes for big name magazines such as *Rolling Stone*, and *The New Yorker*. You can also enjoy his originality by accessing his homepage, Dark Carnival Online.

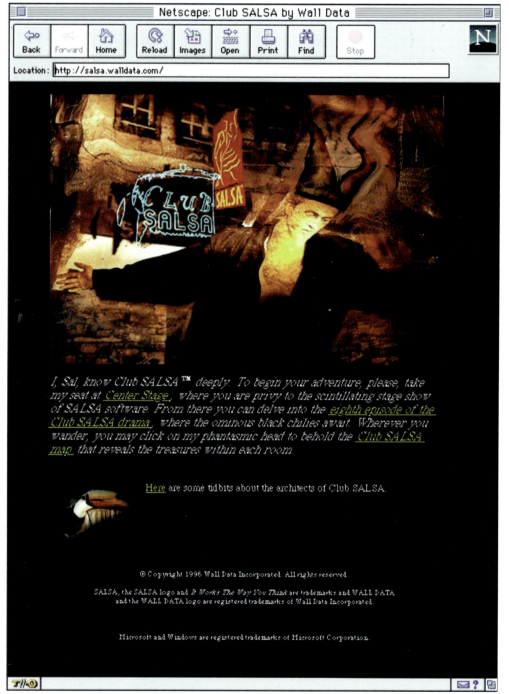

I, Sal, know Club SALSA™ deeply. To begin your adventure, please, take my seat at Center Stage, where you are privy to the scintillating stage show of SALSA software. From there you can delve into the eighth episode of the Club SALSA drama, where the ominous black chilies await. Wherever you wander, you may click on my phantasmic head to behold the Club SALSA map that reveals the treasures within each room.

Here are some tidbits about the architects of Club SALSA.

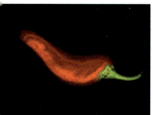

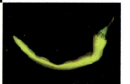

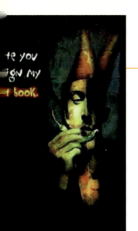

SAL, a hero in a story at the Club. (left)
Club SALSA, a rough sketch of the Club
serving as an index. (Clickable map, below)
In Havana Lounge, a variety of topics of
conversation are leaping between guests.
(Page for software customers, right)

Check out these Rooms in Club Salsa:

What Happened?
The Drama

The SALSA
Products Revue
Center Stage

See How SALSA
Products Do It
Backstage

Meet the SALSA
Product Line
**Lily's Dressing
Rooms**

SALSA Products
Learning Tools
Gaspar's Studio

Online Discussions
and Information
Havana Lounge

Who's Running
This Joint?
Boss' Office

The Latest News
and Gossip
La Clavé Bar

Sneak Previews
The Alley

Past Events
at Club SALSA
Alonzo's Attic

Nearby Hot Spots
Back Door

Bands cannot be missed in a club. Latin music
tunes resound through the Club tonight. (Index
menu page, above)
Stage.(Page presenting products, left)

www.kinotrope.com/ ANNET/menuJ.html

Annet's Cosmic Gei-Cen

(http://www.kinotrope.com/ANNET/menuJ.html)

Design/Production Firm : Kinotrope, Inc.

Client : Kinotrope, Inc.

Art Director : Koji Ito

Creative Director : Koji Ito

Copywriter : Koji Ito

Designer : Misako Aono

Sound : Koji Ito

HTMLwriter : Koji Ito

Programmer : Toshimi Aoki, Akiya Hayashi

This is the site for Gei-Cen (game center) originally produced by Kinotrope, Inc., After all the complicated explanation by Ito, a creative director, regarding database of server's side, etc, I came to the conclusion that there are very few homepages besides this one where so much time and effort were used. I picked this site precisely because the whole package consists of Shockwave files. There is not much to say about its layout of texts, which is easy to understand. Users may well find its set-up interesting, especially that of daily lives of the heroine Annet Saito and her family. The design of the sections and the games they include are also enjoyable. Users may happen to recognize the name of the section "Gravity's Rainbow" as the same title of a novel by Thomas Vinchon. The producer is devoted to design and production of the site of its extreme.

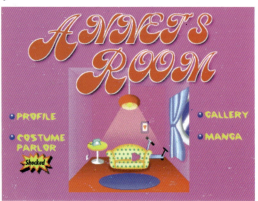

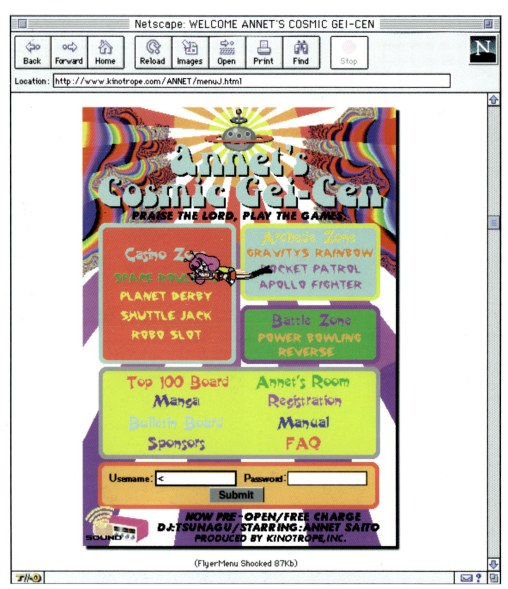

(FlyerMenu Shocked 87Kb)

Primary colors are used in a wide range, including games and graphic parts, to facilitate easier data compression and file transfer. I leave it to your discretion whether this homepage interests you or not, but I hope that you try to play some...

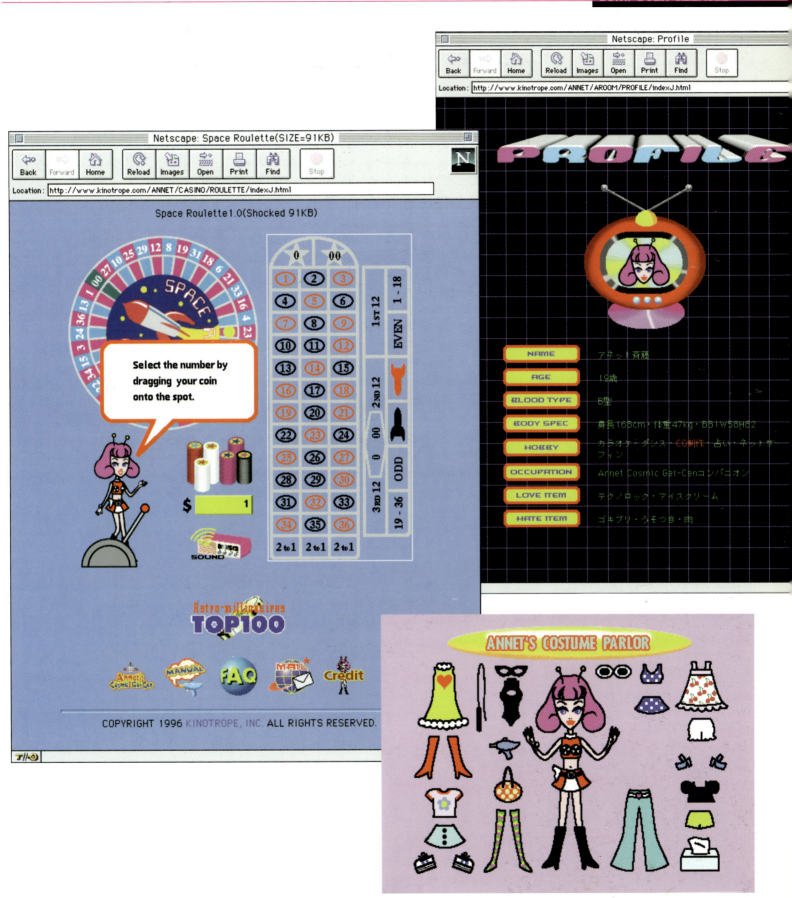

art.redstar.com

Art Technology Group, Inc.

(http://art.redstar.com)

Design/Production Firm : Art Technology Group, Inc.

Art Technology Group, Inc., established five years ago by graduates of MIT Media Labo, is an growing and energetic software company. Having well-known clients such as MCI Telecom, Gemini Consulting, Chiat/Day Advertising, and Apple Computer, they make a specialty of database system. This homepage is divided into one page describing the company and its business - ATG page; and another presenting their products-DYNAMO page.

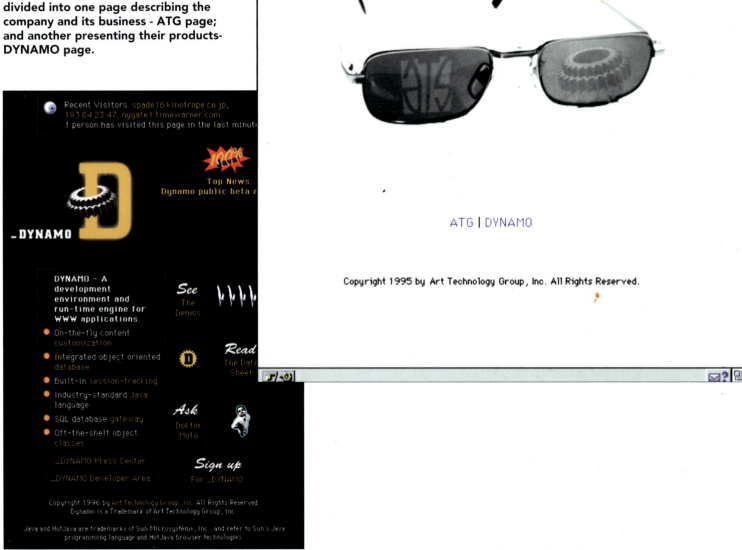

www.netoutfit.com

Internet Outfitters

(http://www.netoutfit.com)

A number of images of airplanes, compasses, and maps are seen throughout this site. The verb outfit means to prepare for an exploratory flight. The title and design of this homepage indicate that it was intended to help an explorer (client) prepare for the Internet world. Viewers will find a picture of an airplane at the top left corner of the front page, where the background changes in concert with the rotation of a propeller. This was designed with extra modification of GIF animation. Elaborate arrangements can be seen in other aspects, such as the

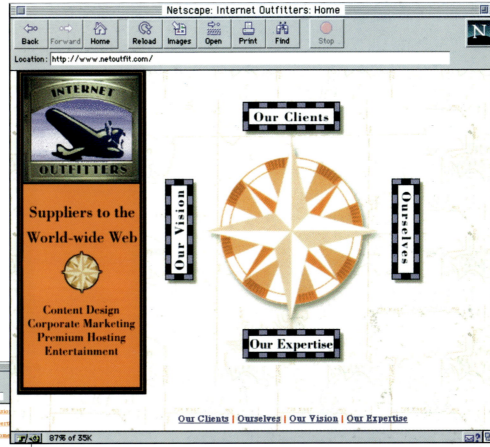

color of text being the same orange color as that of th compass. It is no wonder that they have Toshiba US and other well-known companies as clients, as this "Outfitters" makes good preparations for explorers.

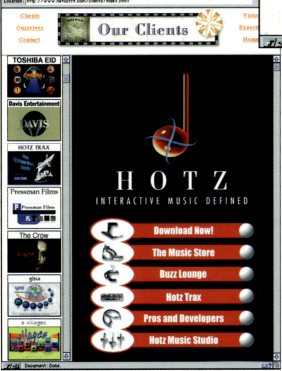

www.ArmaniExchange.com

Armani Exchange

(http://www.ArmaniExchange.com)

Armani Exchange is a diffusion brand of Giorgio Armani. That's only what you would expect of the site of the top fashion designer. The design of each page is simple and chic with consistent colors; black, white and gold. On each page, black and white pictures of young couples are displayed, making the site very fashionable. To control the layout of the texts, they are treated as graphic data. Furthermore, to make the variations of the visual images, server push, client pull and GIF animation are used effectively. In the section of INSPIRATIONS, you can see Armani's advice for living.

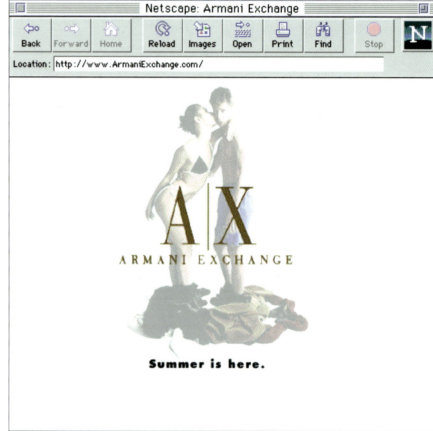

The first page where client pull is used. Firstly, a picture of a young couple wearing coats appears, and then a picture of them taking off their coats and wearing bathing suits, and finally a picture of them kissing with the message, "Summer is here".

STYLE

Netscape: STYLE

Back | Forward | Home | Reload | Images | Open | Print | Find | Stop

Location: http://www.armaniexchange.com/style.html

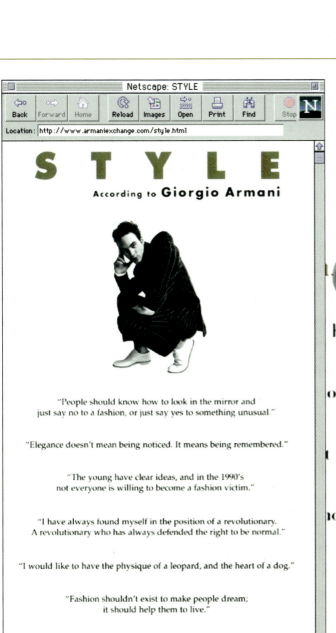

S T Y L E

According to **Giorgio Armani**

"People should know how to look in the mirror and just say no to a fashion, or just say yes to something unusual."

"Elegance doesn't mean being noticed. It means being remembered."

"The young have clear ideas, and in the 1990's not everyone is willing to become a fashion victim."

"I have always found myself in the position of a revolutionary. A revolutionary who has always defended the right to be normal."

"I would like to have the physique of a leopard, and the heart of a dog."

"Fashion shouldn't exist to make people dream; it should help them to live."

menu   inspire

Document : Done.

It's gotta come from somewhere. In

highlight a few of the many things

o art to film to, well, pretty much

t have turned on Mr. Armani lately.

nd get a little inspired, why don't you.

inspire

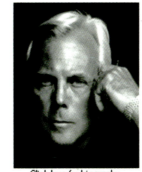

Click here for biography.

You've no doubt seen Giorgio Armani's creations. But have you ever wondered what inspires his signature style? The following is a look behind the scenes into the life of Armani himself. As you'll see, dressing well requires a head, not just a body.

STYLE

FOOD

MUSIC

FILM

menu

www.benetton.com

UNITED COLORS OF BENETTON.

United Colors of Benetton

(http://www.benetton.com)

Benetton is an image conscious clothes manufacturer famous for its sensational advertising campaigns. The site is full of colorful graphic images. It is divided into five sections, BENETTON, PRODUCT, ADVERTISING, COLORS and FABRICA, and each section is classified with different colors. The layout of each page follows the same pattern and the same graphic parts are used on each page so that each is consistent. The site is also full of information. The album of photographs of the latest advertising campaign featuring Indians was the most impressive.

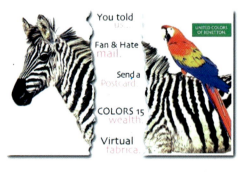

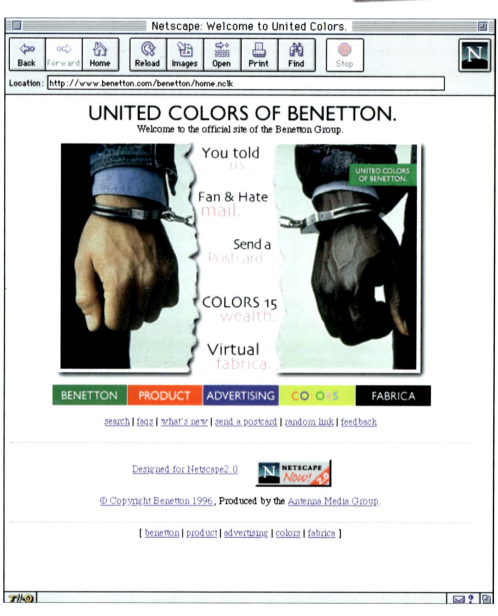

The graphic menu. Every time you access the site, one of ten images of the posters of past ad campaigns appears randomly. (upper)

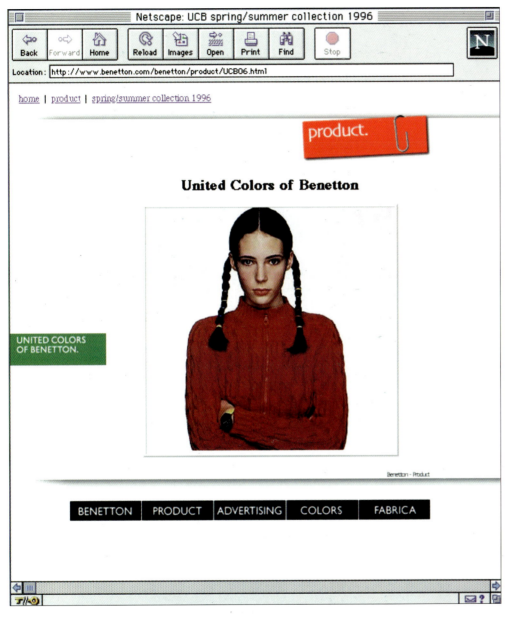

home | product | spring/summer collection 1996

United Colors of Benetton

UNITED COLORS OF BENETTON.

Benetton - Product

| BENETTON | PRODUCT | ADVERTISING | COLORS | FABRICA |

COLOR, DESIGN AND QUALITY.

| BENETTON | PRODUCT | ADVERTISING | COLORS | FABRICA |

The site full of impressive images reminds us of high-quality catalogues. The stock of images are used effectively.

FABRICA.

intro | explain! | evidence | press articles - coming soon!

| BENETTON | PRODUCT | ADVERTISING | COLORS | FABRICA |

www.sisley.com

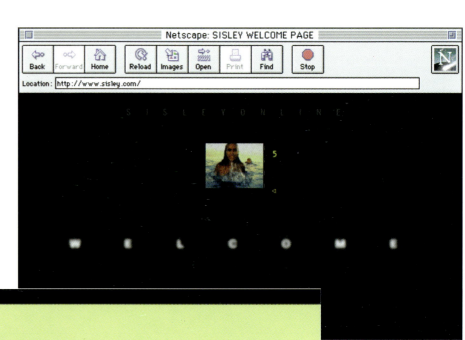

SISLEY
(http://www.sisley.com)

Production : Giorgio Galli & Partners Communications
Website Operation : Starlink Italia

SISLEY is a sister brand of Benetton. This site reminds me that apparel makers sell their images. On the first page you can see a slide show of a woman jumping up from the sea and the word "WELCOME". Black and white headings and the dark navy line at the bottom of each page give a consistent image to all the pages. The background color is different on each page. It is a vivid and fashionable homepage, as good as Benetton's.

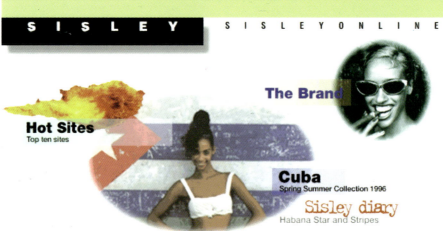

Who is the woman in the slide show? The answer is in the section of Advertising. The theme of SISLEY's advertising campaign was Havana, Cuba this year and Yuly was its main character. (right) You can download 30 second TV CM featuring Yuly and her diary. (bottom left)

SISLEY SISLEYONLINE
Products

Spring Summer 96
NO FRAMES

H O M E
- Back

- Men's Collection
- Lady's Collection

- Jeans
- Eyewear

- Shoes & Accessories
- Beachwear

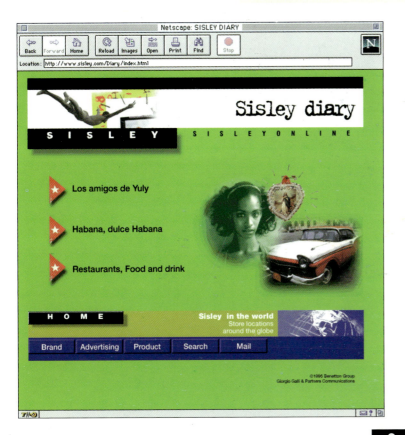

www.levi.com

Levis

(http://www.levi.com)

Production : Organic Online

The site with moving graphic images targets the youth market. Youths must say that this site is cool. The graphic images and typography are modern, for example, images of denim and buttons are used as the icons. In the section of Inner Seam*E.U.*Washroom, you can see the black and white server push movie and TV commercial. The pages show the street fashion and culture from all over the world, including a report about Shibuya and Harajuku in Tokyo. It is interesting to see what people from other countries think about Japanese fashion and culture. The site is often updated.

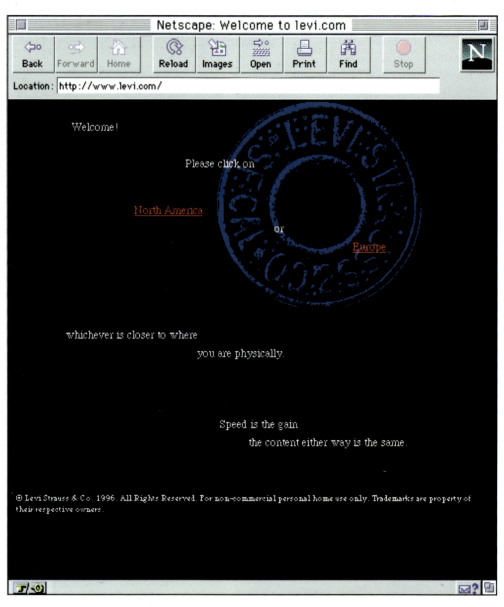

The Girl
The Young Guy
The Blind Man
The Director

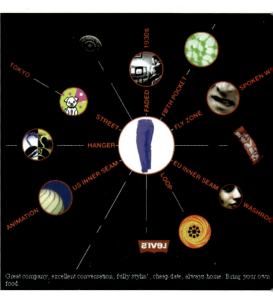

Back Forward Home Reload Images Open Print Find Stop

Location: http://www.levi.com/inner-seam/eu/

Magic Painting

01 Zone

Washroom

Spaceman

Welcome to the European Inner-Seam

In the Vault:
Clayman

Washroom

"It's 3:00 a.m.

Story

"I reach over and turn on the radio. It coughs up a noise that reminds me of a soundtrack to a bad dream.

Music

"The rain is hitting my windshield so hard, I can barely hear the tinny garbled voices. The cars outside rush by like falling elevators.

Movie

"My headlights catch fleeting images of ghostly faces, pressed up against glass in silent desperation. I'm lost in the middle of nowhere.

Cast

But I keep my eyes on the road, and I don't look back."

Falling Elevators,
Welcome to My Dream
MC 900 Ft. Jesus

Test your Bra Muscle

Play a game, save a screen.

New **Prize** alert! Fill in the mi
letters using the little drawings as c
right and you'll win the latest Le
screen saver designed with Love
who couldn't stand a little m
So click **Play** and log in please. W
promise not to sell or hand out a
information you give us. We just wa
who's out there.

Example

s   r e e

play game

European version of Inner-Seam. There are two
versions: European and American. (left)
The Server Push movie, Washroom. (right)

www.ralphlaurenfragrance com

Ralph Lauren Fragrance

(http://www.ralphlaurenfragrance.com)

Production : razorfish

This is the first site provided by Ralph Lauren. It is designed by razorfish, a design production firm on the East coast that has designed the sites of American Online (AOL), Microsoft, IBM and Sony. So, I have great expectations of the site. The first page is server push animation, and it is divided by color into four sections, red, yellow, white and blue. On the page of "rl fragrance", varieties of the products are displayed; "connections" is communication space for the chat program, using the program named Palace; on the page of "the pulse", you can watch an original serial drama; and "ralph lauren" shows the company's history and information. "the pulse" is an original multimedia serial drama featuring five young people, Julia, Kate, Peter, Zach and Mark. It uses the structure of Hyper-Text and links with "rl fragrance" and "connections". The very wide table of the company history on "ralph lauren" has an impact. The images somewhat lack sharpness, but the site is enjoyable and has a lot of graphic images.

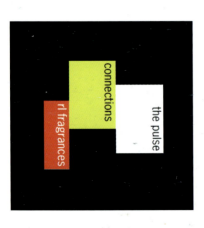

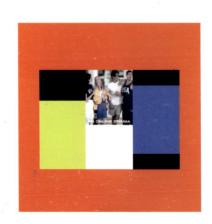

Server push animation on the first page. If you use computers with fast modems and CPUs, you will see various images quickly. (left)

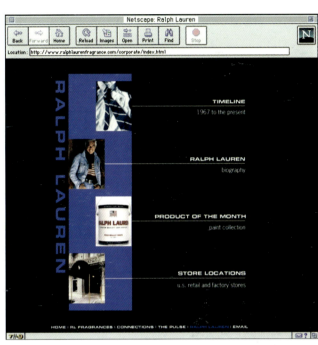

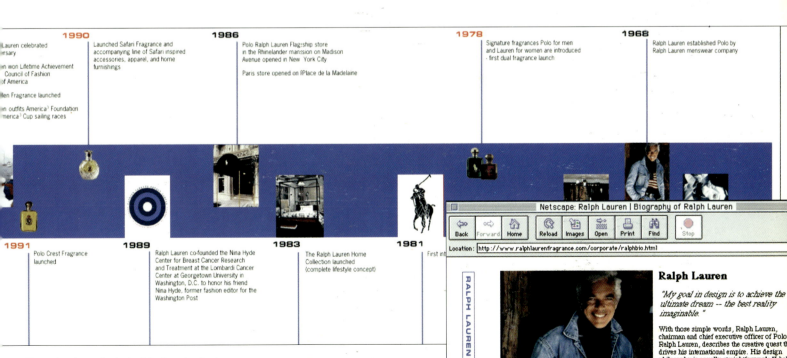

1990	**1986**		**1978**	**1968**
Lauren celebrated ...rsary	Launched Safari Fragrance and accompanying line of Safari inspired accessories, apparel, and home furnishings	Polo Ralph Lauren Flagship store in the Rhinelander mansion on Madison Avenue opened in New York City	Signature fragrances Polo for men and Lauren for women are introduced - first dual fragrance launch	Ralph Lauren established Polo by Ralph Lauren menswear company
...en won Lifetime Achievement ...Council of Fashion ...of America		Paris store opened on fPlace de la Madelaine		
...len Fragrance launched				
...in outfits America³ Foundation ...merica³ Cup sailing races				

1991	**1989**		**1983**	**1981**
Polo Crest Fragrance launched	Ralph Lauren co-founded the Nina Hyde Center for Breast Cancer Research and Treatment at the Lombardi Cancer Center at Georgetown University in Washington, D.C. to honor his friend Nina Hyde, former fashion editor for the Washington Post		The Ralph Lauren Home Collection launched (complete lifestyle concept)	First int...

From the chronological table that details the company's 30-year history, we can see that Ralph Lauren is both verry up-to-date and long-established. (upper)

Ralph Lauren

"My goal in design is to achieve the ultimate dream -- the best reality imaginable."

With those simple words, Ralph Lauren, chairman and chief executive officer of Polo Ralph Lauren, describes the creative quest that drives his international empire. His design philosophy is equally straightforward: "I believe in design that has integrity, design that lasts. Whatever it is, it must be part of the lifestyle become more personal with time."

Since he first introduced Polo men's ties in 1967, Mr. Lauren's work has come to represent the best of American design. His name, synonymous with natural elegance and enduring style, has shaped the way people dress and live. Renowned internationally, Mr. Lauren's influence has spread beyond fashion into the worlds of advertising, interior design and retailing.

Ferrari

(http://www.ferrari.it/ferrari)

The official web site of Ferrari is a remarkably tasteful homepage. It is an on-line catalogue based on the actual print catalogue. The design of the cover page is a 3D silver logo with the emblem of a horse on a Italian red background. The next page is a preface with the comments of Enzo Ferrari. These are displayed with a sepia photograph of young Ferrari and two icons of keys with the images of the flags of Italy and England, by which you can choose the language in which you want to go on. The site offers sections called History, Models, Racing, Oggetti Ferrari, Ferrari Club, Guest Book and News, each full of useful information. The well balanced layout conveys an aura of nobility. If the designer had not been an Italian, authentic Italian taste might not have been created—as Roman Holiday is Hollywood's sense of Italy even though some of the scenes take place in Rome. If you visit the site, you will feel the true and great artistic power of Italian culture. It is worth visiting even if you are not interested in Ferraris or other cars. The logo of Telecom Italia is displayed throughout the site so that it seems to be produced in cooperation with them. Perhaps, such a wonderful site may not have been created without cooperation between two leading Italian companies.

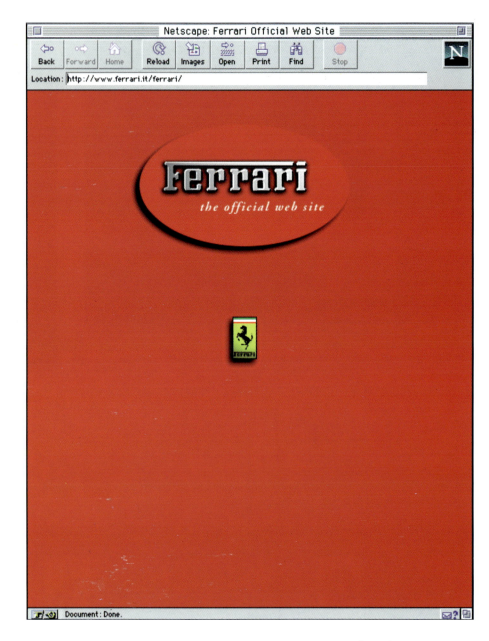

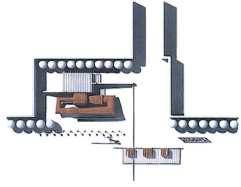

 History

 Models

 Racing

 Oggetti Ferrari

 Ferrari Club

 Guest Book

 News

Netscape: Ferrari Benvenuto/Welcome

Location: http://www.ferrari.it/ferrari/frontesp.html

Molta gente importante mi invita ad andare in questa o quella città. Io rispondo che non vado perché vedrebbero me, un uomo come un altro. Li invito invece a venire a Maranello perché qui possono vedere come facciamo le nostre macchine e parlare anche con i miei collaboratori.

Many important people invite me to go to this or that city. I respond that I do not go because they would see me, a man like any other. Instead, I invite them to come to Maranello because here they can see how we make our cars and they can also talk with my collaborators.

Enzo Ferrari

TELECOM ITALIA
a STET Company

PARTNER TECNOLOGICO DELLA FERRARI ©

© Ferrari S.p.A. The total or partial reproduction of text, photographs and illustrations is not permitted in any form.

Info

Document: Done.

A photograph of young Enzo Ferrari. The two keys mean the beginning of the homepage. (upper)

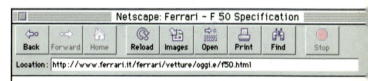

Netscape: Ferrari – F 50 Specification

Location: http://www.ferrari.it/ferrari/vetture/oggi.e/f50.html

Ferrari F 50

This was built to the same criteria as a F1 car, adapted to the demands of road driving, and was the fruit of research carried out by an experienced manufacturer who has designed and built 45 racing models and innumerable GT and Sport models. The engine-gearbox-differential assembly, of F1 origin, supports the rear axle assembly and is fastened to the carbon fibre chassis. The body is in carbon fibre composite, to bring out the car's sporty personality and is available in two versions: a Berlinetta with integral hardtop, and a Barchetta, with an aerodynamic element incorporating two anti-roll safety bars attached to the chassis.

Dimensions and Weights

Length	176.4 in
Width	78.2 in
Height	44.1 in

www.psa.fr

PSA Peugeot Citroen

(http://www.psa.fr)

Design/Production : CARRE NOIR

The yellowish color used in the background is the biggest attraction of this site. Such soft and warm colors can be created only by designers with a sophisticated sense of color, like the French perhaps. The fading borderline between the white and yellow are designed with much care. Off course, the French tricolor are also used. The overall impression of the surroundings is very special. The dark red is the accent color of the design. The designs of some web sites reflect cultural backgrounds. By the way, I saw the same red car as the one on the site, running in the venue of a summit meeting in Lyons. It was one of the promotional activities by Peugeot, which was one of the sponsors of the meeting.

In addition to the color effect, the layout of the images and texts and humorous expressions convey a French flavor.

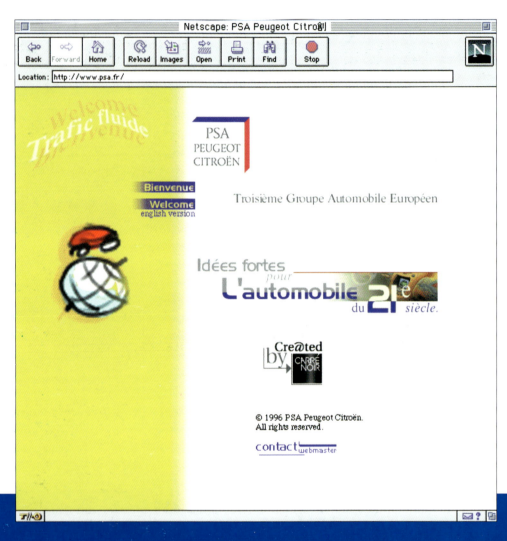

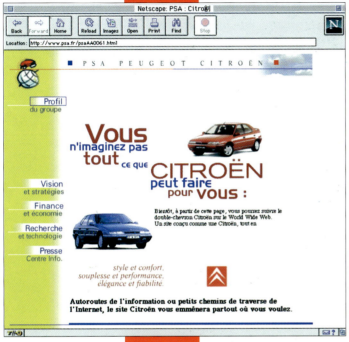

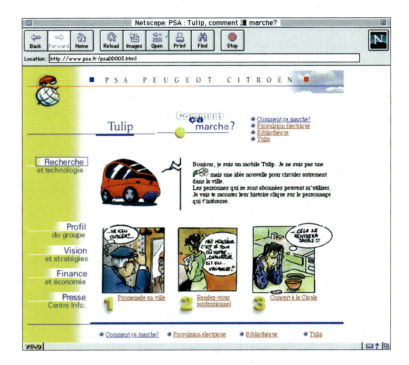

Organisation

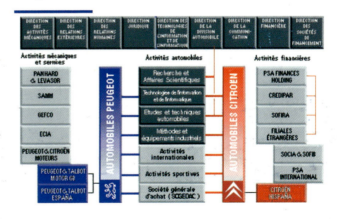

Le dialogue de la science et de la technologie

Tulip :
Concept de mobilité urbaine

Dossiers Recherche
- Propulsion électrique
- Bibliothèque

www.saabusa.com

Saab USA

(http://www.saabusa.com)

The impressive illustration of this homepage was done by a famous designer who also did the label of a local beer. Although the site offers information on the company and its products as other motor companies do, because of the illustration this creates an unusual feeling. This is not to say that major motor companies like GM and FORD should follow this type of homepage. The site is designed to entertain the visitors by its illustration, which matches the image of the company's products. Incidentally, in the US, Saab was popular among yuppies in 1980's. More devices and sensibility are needed for the sites of image-conscious companies like motor and fashion companies than are needed for their advertising imprint media.

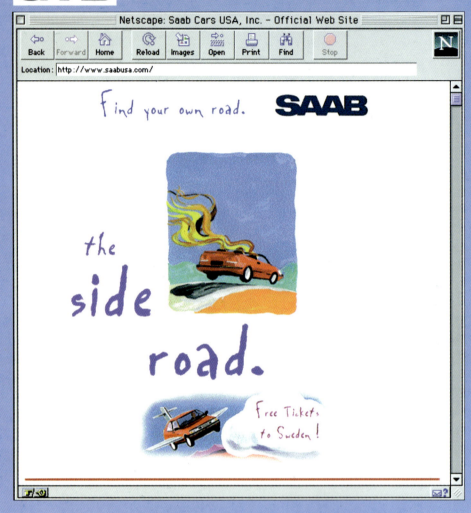

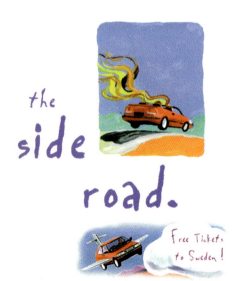

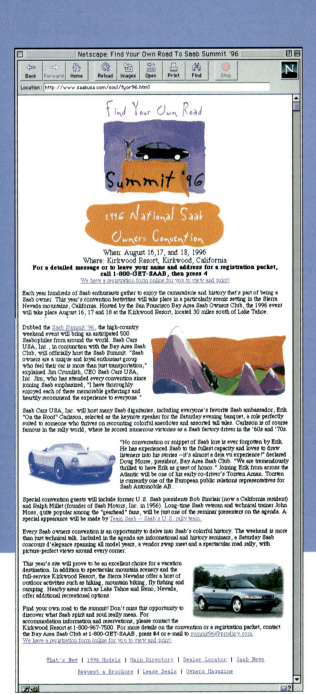

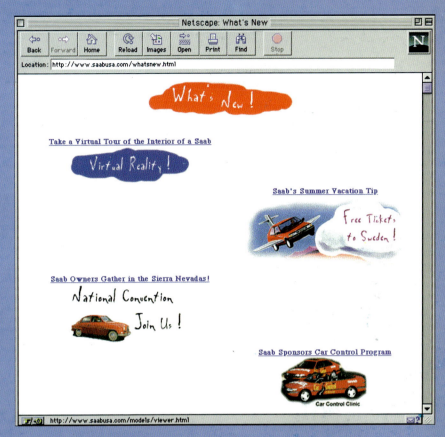

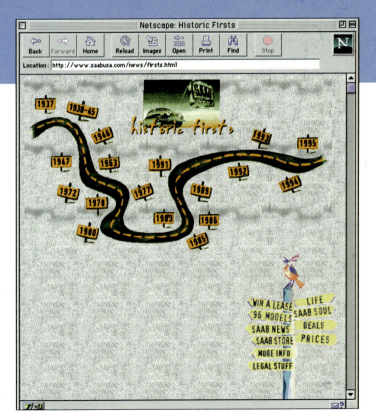

The page of Owners Convention. (upper)
What's New in simple layout. (upper right)
The page on company history. Does the winding
road mean that the company had many twists and
turns? (right bottom)

www.bmwusa.com

BMW of North America

(http://www.bmwusa.com)

This is the site of BMW of North America. Most homepages of foreign firms in Japan are merely Japanese translations of the contents used by the firms' headquarters, such that they somewhat appear awkward to us. Well-known companies should have high-quality homepages, since it reflects their attitude of doing business on the Internet. BMW USA is the site used for a TV commercial of Apple Computer in June, 1996. The site is full of multi-media displays, rich with animation and sound effects. It also has interactive services, including a section where you can design your own BMW. Moreover, the consistent adherence to the corporate image makes this site an exemplary one indeed.

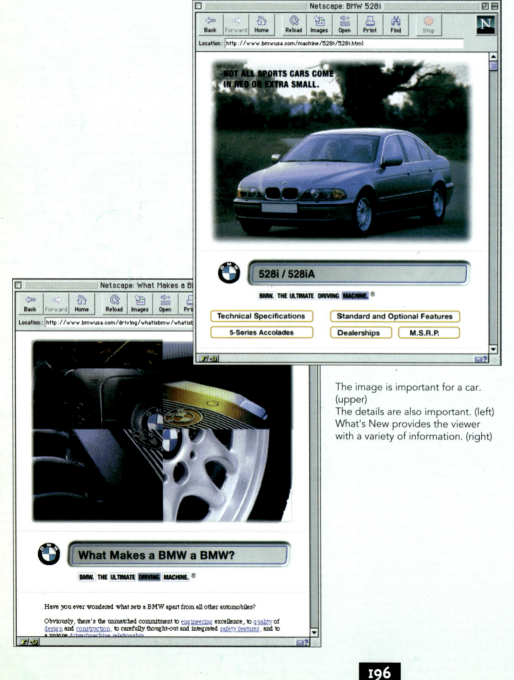

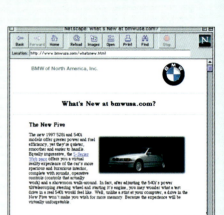

The image is important for a car. (upper)
The details are also important. (left)
What's New provides the viewer with a variety of information. (right)

www.american express.com

American Express Inc.
(http://www.americanexpress.com)

The most notable point of this site is its illustrations, especially those used in the section of American Express University, which remind use of comic book. Such unexpected casualness from a conservable card company may be a clear indication that this site is geared towards the core of net users, namely, the younger generation. Nonetheless, the company's flexibility is refreshing. The site is divided into sections for various travel services offered to card holders. American Express University targets students using an amusing icon, a Roman soldier, the company's trade mark, wearing dark glasses.

www.bofa.com

Bank of America

(http://www.bofa.com)

Bank of America, which is the most notable bank on the west coast, appeared on the Web much earlier than other banks and has been providing a good amount of information. When I accessed its site December 1994, I was happy to see that it had been updated for Christmas. Its present site is a typical American corporate site. The images used for the front page menu, headings of solid figures on each page and the icons, are typical American designs. The contents of the site are also well organized with much useful information, including the company information, their business services, the latest economic and financial news and their activities for the environment. And in the section of HomeBanking, you can check the balance of your account and make remittances. Nowadays, in Japan on-line banking is discussed a lot, but no bank has started the service yet. I can feel the pioneering spirit from these American home pages, which have been developed by producing a lot of experimental homepages. This is similar to the process of the development of the Internet.

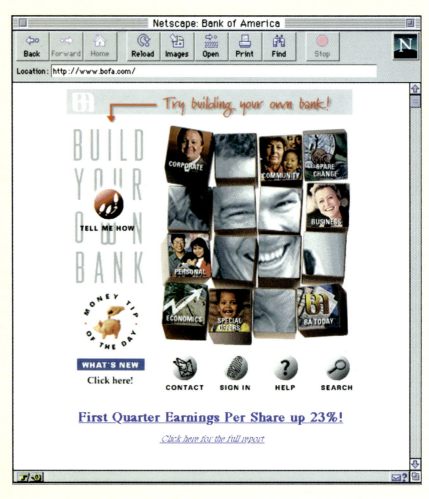

The graphical menu consists of icons of various peoples' faces. (upper)
The page of introducing their services. (left)
The page of Bank of America art collection in the section of "Spare Change". (right)

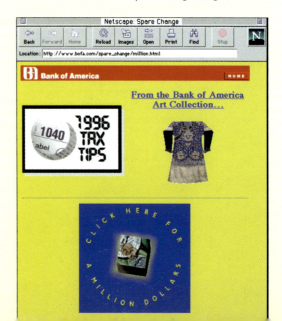

wellsfargo.com

WELLS FARGO

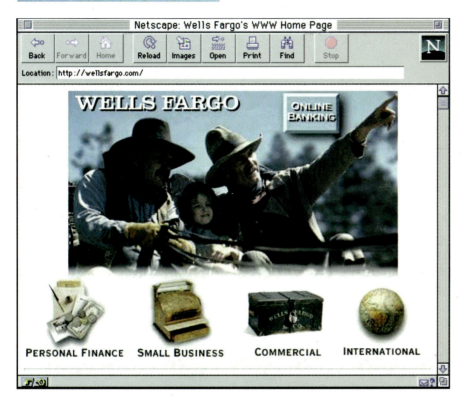

Wells Fargo

(http://wellsfargo.com)

A good rivalry in the same town, such as the college football powerhouses UCLA and USC, is called a cross-town rival. Wells Fargo is one of the leading banks based in San Francisco where the Bank of America mentioned in the page before, is also based. So the relationship between these two companies can be called a cross-town rival. Wells Fargo's logo is a stagecoach, and motifs, depicting the American West and California gold rush are used in many pages. The company's contributions to the development of San Francisco are mentioned in the section called About Wells Fargo. You can also find information about the historical museum named after the company on the page of the gallery. Pioneer, which is the theme throughout the visual images on the site, must be a witty metaphor of the bank near Silicon Valley where there are many computer companies that develop on-line systems called "the cyber frontier". The visual image is designed well with the backgrounds in chic colors and elaborately designed icons.

www.stoli.com

![STOLI logo]

Stoli Central

(http://www.stoli.com)

This is the site of Stolichnaya, a vodka which has been popular throughout the world for a long time. This site was created by the American importer of Stolichnaya, and its slogan is "Freedom of Vodka". So, "Freedom" is used as a key word through the whole site. The first page is a graphic menu with visual images, like Russian avant-garde, where the titles of some sections including the word "Freedom" are placed. The site also includes pages for fun. For example, STOLI NOTE is a page where you can select and send your favorite post cards adding your personal messages while in FREEDOM OF EXPRESSION, you can put your own colors on the drawing of a bottle and download its GIF images. Besides these, the site offers various interesting pages including one with posters designed for Stolichnaya and another one introducing recipes for a variety of cocktails made with Stolichnaya. This site is innovative and highly enjoyable.

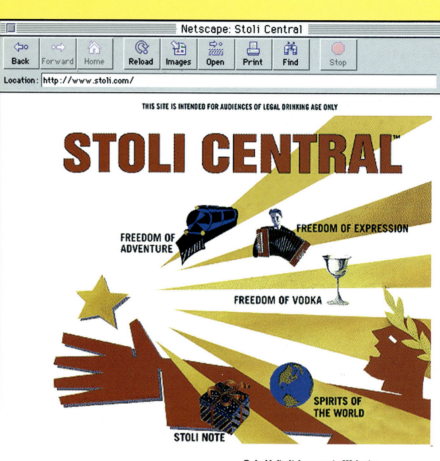

Behold Stolichnaya(R)'s Web site with a twist -- the only stop on the Internet where you can be creator and critic, be in Moscow and Mexico, as well as become bemused, befuddled and benevolent all in a single visit. That's because at STOLI CENTRAL freedom reigns supreme.

So if you've yet to do so, add the site to your personal hotlist to stay on top of all the latest.

STOLI (™) NOTE

Whether it's a rollicking "Happy Birthday" or a simple "Howdy-doo," STOLI CENTRAL (™) has everything you need to design and send your very own electronic greeting cards.

FREEDOM OF EXPRESSION

Go out of your mind solving the Stoli Cipher. Stay in the lines as you brandish the Stoli Palette. And if you're not quite getting the picture at the Stoli Gallery, the Stoli Translator will help put it into words.

FREEDOM OF VODKA(™)

Be the bartender, a cocktail critic or both. The freedom is yours. Just make sure not

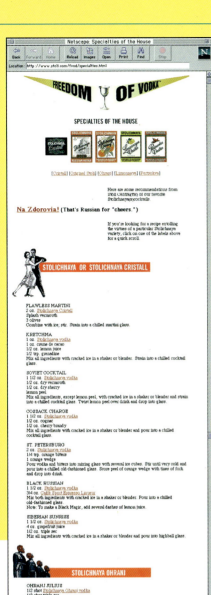

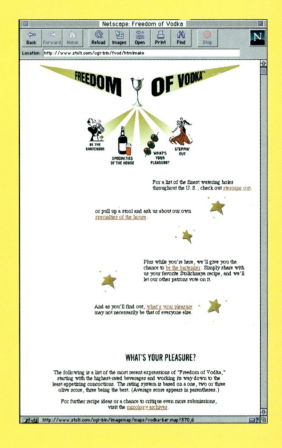

The pages of the recipes of various Stolichnaya cocktails. (left)
The page of Stoli Translator, where you can translate the word Freedom into various languages. (center)

Netscape: View Your Card

Location: http://www.stoli.com:80/cgi-bin/notes/choosebg.pl?note-ad2.GIF

Here is your charming selection in its actual size:

Now it's time to add your personal message.

FAQ & e-mail / Table of Contents

(21 & OLDER)

The page of STOLI NOTE, on which your favorite
image of the posters can be sent as an electronic post
card with your personal message. (left)
The page of SPIRITS OF THE WORLD. Incidentally,
Bombay Sapphire is one of the world's finest gin as
popular as Tanqueray. (right)

Netscape: Spirits of the World: Bombay Sapphire Gin

Location: http://www.stoli.com/cgi-bin/lingo/bombay-sapphire.html

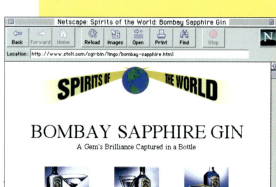

SPIRITS OF THE WORLD

BOMBAY SAPPHIRE GIN
A Gem's Brilliance Captured in a Bottle

A precious stone of such unequalled brilliance that it remains the Indian subcontinent's most celebrated jewel, the Bombay sapphire is a fitting namesake for one of the world's most distinctive gins. Thanks to Carillon Importers Ltd., Bombay Sapphire Gin, the fastest growing gin in America, is available throughout the U.S. to gin connoisseurs for whom no well-appointed bar would be complete without this quintessentially British spirit.

The Botanicals of Bombay Sapphire

Delectably dry Bombay Sapphire Gin owes its singularly exquisite taste to a delicate combination of no less than ten natural botanicals (the most of any gin). Each of these botanical ingredients, including grains of paradise, almonds, lemon peel, licorice, juniper berries, cubeb berries, orris, coriander, angelica and cassia bark, adds a distinctive and complementary facet to this gem of gins.

This fortuitous mixture and a slow double-distillation process produce a 94-proof, 100-percent grain-neutral spirit that lives up to its esteemed reputation as the world's finest gin.

Packaged in an elegant blue bottle engraved on two sides with its ten rare botanicals, Bombay Sapphire is available in 1L and 50ml sizes, and 750ml and 1.75L deluxe gift boxes, allowing the right size gem for any occasion.

STOLI CENTRAL   (21 & OLDER)

[Stoli Central][To Order (21 & Older)]

FAQ & e-mail / Table of Contents

c 1996 Carillon Importers, Ltd., Teaneck, NJ.

Document: Done.

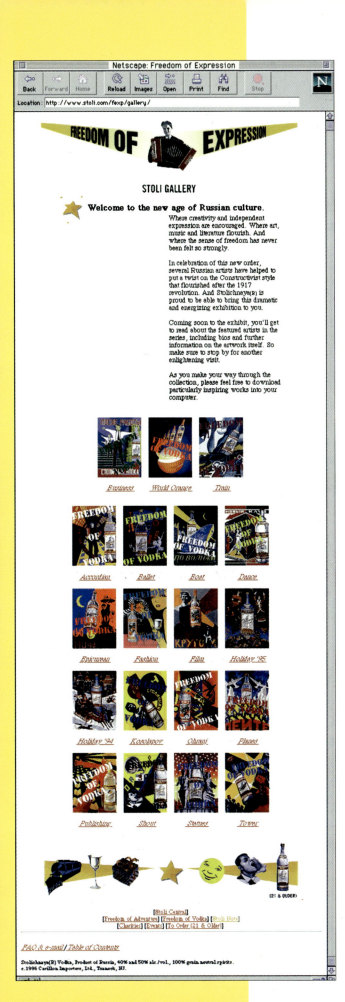

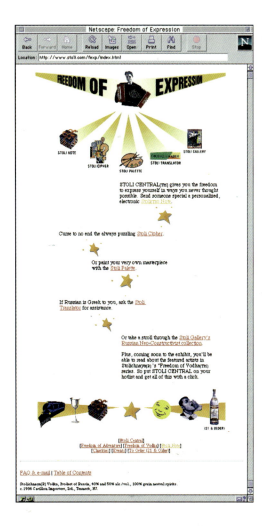

Posters displayed on STOLI GALLERY. (left)
Palettes for coloring. (bottom)

The freedom is yours.

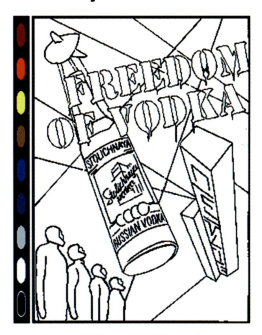

www.guinness.ie

Guinness

(http://www.guinness.ie)

This is the site of a world wide famous stout brand Guinness. Guinness is an Irish brew popular among those who love its unique flavor. The backgrounds of the pages are basically black like the color of the stout, and there are two main sections. One is "VISIT THE LOCAL", which is black and white. The idea is that you can visit a pub on line without leaving your house. Every time you access this section, first you see the pages with various messages at random. For example, one of the messages is quoted from the words of Pete Townsend, a member of the rock band The WHO, that is "I would rather die than get old." These messages differentiate this site from ones that only promote their products. And also the message written at the bottom of each page "Not Everything in Black and White Makes Sense" is a mature comment, like the image of black color of Guiness. This section includes a quote of the month titled "Whom Do You Want to Impress ?" and a collection of Web site links recommended by a bartender called Leonardo.

The section titled VISIT THE BREWERY is an imaginary brewery where you can learn about Guinness; its company history, the system of brewing, etc. There are also some quiz pages, where you can learn about the process of brewing, from the ingredients of the brew to the fixing of the brewing period, by answering questions. This section consists of interactive pages designed by using software like Shockwave. On the first page the gate of the brewery opens, and then each bubble inside the gate (incidentally, the bubble is one of the symbols of Guinness beer) leads you to each page. This gives you the feeling that you are actually going through the gate. The combination of gold and red on the plain black backgrounds is beautiful. In order to design attractive web sites for the food and bevarage industry, which is rather not related to computers or their networks, it is important to have good tricks and metaphorical images. With that in consideration, that, this site is one of the best.

www.perrier.com

Perrier

(http://www.perrier.com)

The site is subtitled "The Art of Refreshment" and is full of colorful and fancy illustrations. The design of this site is one of my favorites. The artistic design is most impressive. Many net/web sites are designed with high-tech gimmicks like 3D, but this one has fancy and warm graphics. The texts are written in lime-green, Perrier's color and is coordinated with the color of graphic images. The page of Art Gallery could not have been made without the long history of the company. It shows the posters of Perrier of each period, designed by famous artists of Art decor, Impressionism and Cubism. And if you open the page, Bottle Gallery, you can see the designs of original Perrier bottles and you will also be able to design your own bottles. There is also a page of recommended restaurants. This site, so full of stories and tips about eating, art, and amusement can really be called the epitome of French taste.

Welcome to www.perrier.com, where The Art of Refreshment comes to life! During your visit, Pierre invites you to dance among each of our featured sections.

Enter the Perrier Great Serve Sweepstakes and Win a Trip to the French Open and other Great Prizes!

Tennis For exclusive online coverage of the action at Roland Garros stadium, check out Tennis Online, the Web site of *Tennis* magazine. Correspondent Sandra Harwitt is filing stories twice a day, and Professional Sport Photography is supplying photos within hours of court play.

- Enter the Perrier Great Serve Sweepstakes, and you could win a trip for two to the French Open.
- Find your favorite restaurant in **New York, Los Angeles, Chicago, Washington, D.C., and now, New Orleans** with the help of the Gayot's Restaurant Guide.
- Browse through Pierre's Art Gallery.
- Check out what Pierre is wearing in the Catalog.
- Help Pierre get to know you in the Hello section. (You could win a year's supply of Perrier free!)
- If you work in a restaurant , we have a special prize for you.
- Learn about the humble country water that became renowned the world over in the Info section.
- See our latest Art Bottles in the Art Bottles Gallery.
- Be among the first to see the new Perrier bottle art in Winners.
- Take a look at the contest winners in the Winner's Gallery.

Pierre frequently redecorates, so be sure to come back again and again!

(Pierre has designed this site especially for Netscape 1.1)

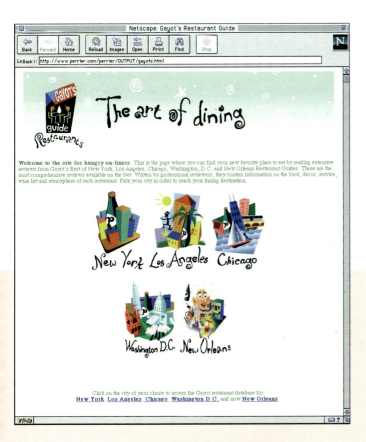

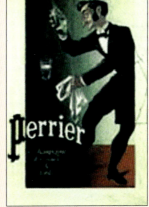

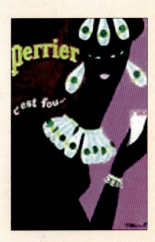

www.sothebys.com

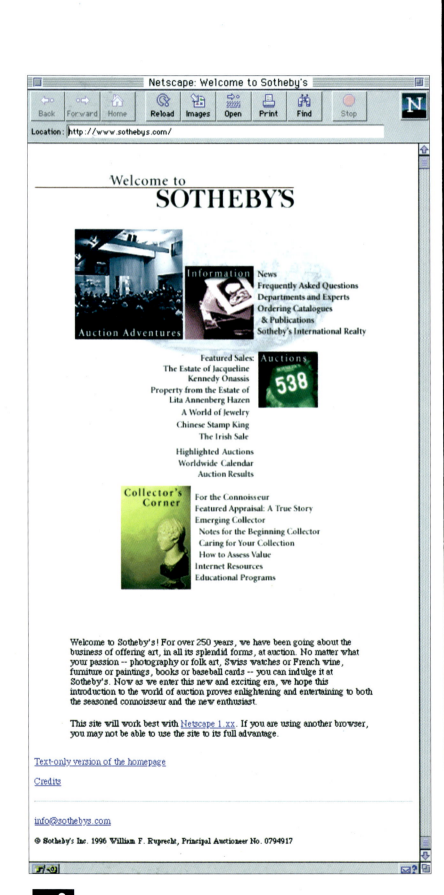

Welcome to

SOTHEBY'S

Sotheby's

(http://www.sothebys.com)

The home page of Sotheby's, a well-known auction company, is finally on the net. It was a recent topic that the estate of Jacqueline Kennedy Onassis was sold through Sotheby's. This article is also on the site. I wanted to see the contents of the site because Sotheby's is not familiar to ordinary people, and I was wondering if they would be able to design a homepage that could appeal to visitors. In fact, the site is organized very well and has a good layout. Especially, the pages related to the auctions are well done. They make it easy to understand the system of auctioning and to see the products. I was also impressed by the details; for example, each section has its own color scheme making navigation through the site smooth.

The images on the first page of the site. The images leading to the pages are good accents to the design of the first page.

INFORMATION

ADVENTURES

AUCTIONS   COLLECTOR

HOME

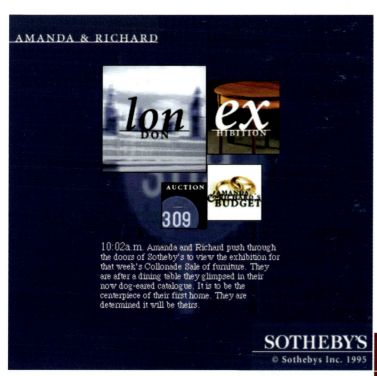

AMANDA & RICHARD

10:02a.m. Amanda and Richard push through the doors of Sotheby's to view the exhibition for that week's Collonade Sale of furniture. They are after a dining table they glimpsed in their now dog-eared catalogue. It is to be the centerpiece of their first home. They are determined it will be theirs.

SOTHEBY'S
© Sothebys Inc. 1995

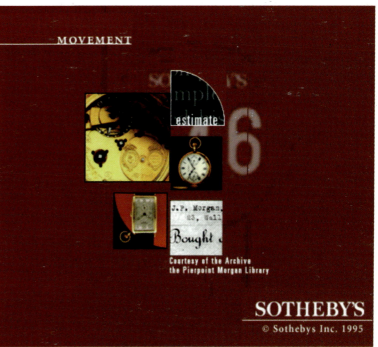

MOVEMENT

Courtesy of the Archive
the Pierpoint Morgan Library

SOTHEBY'S
© Sothebys Inc. 1995

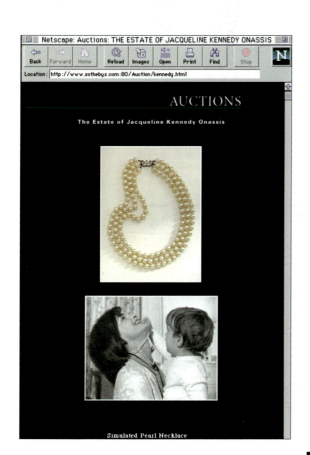

The page of the story of auctions and products.
(upper left & right)
The imitation pearl necklace of Jacqueline
Kennedy wearing it. (bottom left)

www.kinkos.com

Kinko's

(http://www.kinkos.com)

Design/Production Firm :
Hal Riney & Partners Heartland Chicago, IL
Client : Kinko's
Art Director : Stephanie Haumueller
Copywriter : John Kastanes
Designer : Stephanie Haumueller
Programmer : Organic Online

Kinko's is a service bureau called a business convenience store. On the pages of Kinko's Story, you will find the history of the company; in the 1970s, a copy shop was opened by some young college graduates. Over time, the business expanded, the needs of the shop is increased, its services have been diversified because of technological developments. Kinko's was the first business convenience store in Japan. Its services include slide outputs and hourly rentals of rooms equipped for video conferencing. The "products and services" pages, serves as a sort of digital company brochure with colors that give it a clean impression.

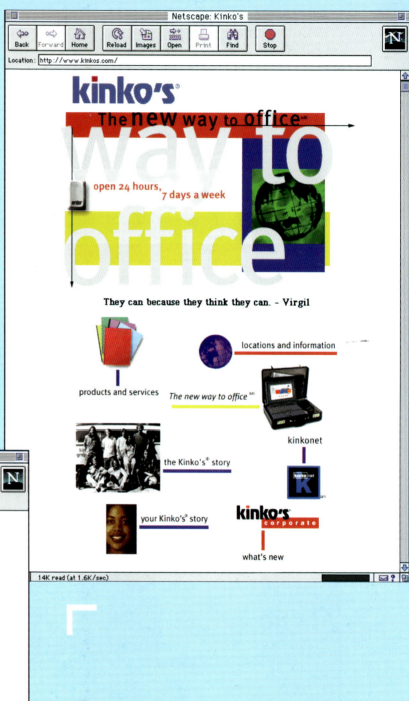

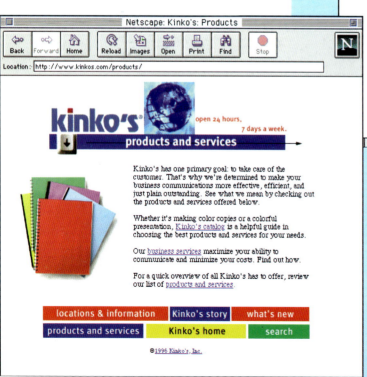

www.polaroid.com

Polaroid

(http://www.polaroid.com)

As may be expected, this home page is designed with much concern about color effects. Very colorful headings with vivid images on every page appeal to viewers. Overall, the site consists of the company's products and services, but there are also some pages for fun. For example, if you open the page named "time machine", you will see a list of the affairs in each era with pictures. Through these pages you can remember the phases of each period while enjoying quizzes related to each era. There are also various pages with beautiful graphic images, such as Replica, Gallery and Test. This site is very well constructed.

www.nystyle.com

NY STYLE

(http://www.nystyle.com)

Design/Production Firm : NYSTYLE, Inc.
Client :
Chetta B, Noviello-Bloom, Region, Get Juiced,
Lindsay Boyer, Robin Rice Galleries, etc.
Art Director :
Sandy di Pasqua (Logo design,Typography)
Debby Koster,Pat Bates (Layout and design)
Creative Director : Debby Koster
Copywriter :
Frieda Bloom, Bernadine Morris, Evelyn Jablow, Dr.
Howard Sobel
Designer : Debby Koster, Pat Bates, Sandy di Pasqua
Illustrator : Sue Rose (Honest Art)
Photographer : Pat Bates, Debby Koster
HTML Writer : Debby Koster, Kenny Hutchinson
Programmer : Kenny Hutchinson
Others :
Scott Matthews (navigation, layouts)
Howard Bloom (Merchandising)

**This site can be called "an on-line catalog
magazine from New York", where the
visitors can actually order products. To
promote the sales of the merchandise,
the designer leaves a lot of blank space
to make the contents clear and to
display the products attractively. And
the pictures themselves of the products
are attractive. We can feel the passion of
the provider. The homepage also
presents a variety of articles related to
lifestyles, including fashion and beauty,
which are updated monthly. All in all, it
looks terrific. We will have to wait and
see, however, how successful it will be.**

Some pages from the shopping catalog. Through this site, you can purchase furniture, accessories and household products. Most of the pictures are of good quality and appeal to the interests of viewers.

by Sylvia Heisel

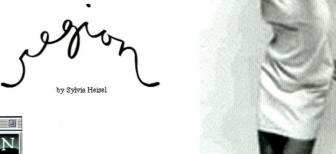

Netscape: Picks of the Month

Back | Forward | Home | Reload | Images | Open | Print | Find | Stop

Location: http://www.nystyle.com/bestbets/index3.htm

shopping

Best Bets
click on images for more details

home
9 to 12
of 12

Mark Zeff Consulting Group featuring the Mark Zeff Collection. Custom-made modern classics. The Safari chair (above) - A curved hot rolled steel frame supports a rattan and wood seat back. A stylish blend of three different materials suitable for any world-weary traveler. - $857

Emerald cross pendant by **Lindsay Boyer Jewelry.** Pendant is pewter with 24K gold plate. Chain is brass with 24K gold plate. Pendant size: 2", 16 1/2" chain. - $45

Hand made tumblers available in vibrant colors by **Jonathan Adler** - $25

The Get Juiced Fasting kit combined with the fasting program draws on ancient methods of rejuvenation of our mental, physical, and spiritual selves. By **Get Juiced**, a popular stop in the Hamptons for fresh juices - $110

Check your basket contents . Check-out . fax order

nystyle   **shopping**   **magazine**   **shopping** *assistance*

Netscape: "Robin Rice Gallery-Girl Sleeping"

Reload | Images | Open | Print | Find | Stop

e.com/rrice/rrstyle3.htm

RICE GALLERY
INE PHOTOGRAPHY

home
3 of 9

"Girl Sleeping" - '88

Signed limited edition of 25
Availability: Unframed: 3 weeks, Framed: 6 weeks.

Framing options (if desired):

Modern step

Traditional slope

Time Flies

No expression other than "Time flies" can describe the developments of the Internet and World Wide Web. Technological innovations are progressing at a dizzying pace and have an ever more immediate effect on daily life. Some say that four months in the real world is equal to one year in cyberspace, and there can be little doubt about it. Indeed, modern society is the stage on which "bitmapped information is racing...wit the seed of light."

On deciding to survey the present stage of development of the Internet and WWW and compile a book might, we editors have, from the very beginning, tried to consider the effect that the book might have on people. The first thing I thought of was that the book is in a way like a time capsule. Because this project was carried out by only a few people, only a few web sites could really be evaluated. In collecting material, we were compelled to rely on chance as we had no URL list corresponding to the theme of the book. First, we accessed the reference site and put bookmarks in the homepages that impressed us. These were chosen randomly by surfing the net. But later, when we had to revisit them in order to write about them, some of the homepages had already been reconstructed, and we had to doublecheck much of the contents. (The homepages in this book are ones that were on the Web between spring and summer 1996.) In any case, capturing homepages and transforming them into printed pages, as we have done for this book, creates the time capsule I spoke of. We have tried to capture the essence of a virtual moment of the constantly changing digital world.

Time capsules are of interest to people of the future, of course, but this book offers a great deal to the people of now as well. It is a wonderful opportunity to those who have never touched a computer and cannot fathom the Internet, read though they might article after article about it. The beautiful homepages that appear in this book must surely excite their interest in the Internet and make them eager to understand it better. The book will also be good for the many Internet users who do not have the time or money to net surf for interesting home pages. They can use it as a shortcut for finding some of the exciting sites. The message that we editors most want to convey to readers, however, concerns the value of positive expression and the importance of visual presentation.

Seeing is believing

As with other forms of digital media, one of the great benefits of the Internet lies in interactive communication; that is, communication that goes beyond mere passive reception. Clearly, the value of the Internet is not that users simply have access to a myriad of information at any time of day or night. In fact, a major media company in the U. S. has launched an experimental project called *Video on Demand*, in which information from many fields is received over the Internet in a passive way, and this project has not met with much success. Communication over the Internet means, rather, that people can actually participate in the making of the communication by expressing opinions or demonstrating artwork. So, people who are not satisfied with entertainment as it is offered by TV or movies should try the Internet, where they can experiment for themselves rather than just assimilate information. And they can communicate with other people who are also experimenting via homepages, or, of course, by using e-mail or chat. It is activities like these that put positive expression into communication, and they have great value.

It's Web that talks

The eye of the Web has become like a window of the soul. Since the Internet, makes interactive communication so easy, more and more people are building up their own homepages and expressing their individuality by making their own URL lists. The Internet is, in a sense, unique because it enables anyone who uses a word processor to build up the mechanisms necessary to use it; and when interesting homepages with appealing layouts are discovered, anyone can take the structures apart and examine them.

There are, however, several points to guard against. One is that the character of the Internet can lead to the overproduction of inferior articles and the unwelcome appearance of amateurish homepages created by individuals and companies from all around the world. Homepages that present a unique atmosphere or reflect personal idiosyncracies tend to fall into this trap less often and so are generally very exciting. Another problem is that it is more difficult now than it was even a year ago for users to reach each others' homepages by chance. So many homepages flow on the Net these days that even the reference and index site has become unhelpful except when people know exactly what to look up. Hopefully, however, we will find ways of overcoming these difficulties.

Now let me turn to what I called the importance of visual presentation. Unless a homepage makes a powerful and immediate impact, people will not be inclined to access its contents or stay long at the site. This is especially true when the screen is filled with text because the attention span of net users tends to be rather short. Creative homepages, however, compel Net-surfers to linger at a site and perhaps become hooked on it. Of course, content and sophisticated programs are important, but considering the vast array of information that must be gone through, greater emphasis ought to be put on the visual elements of any page. Moreover, as more and more users from all around the globe start talking to each other, visual elements will become ever more important as a means of communication.

Copy art to make art

It is most encouraging that many good homepages that can serve as models already exist on the Web, and this book is showcase for some of them. Nonetheless, no matter how long and hard you look at images on a printed page, you will never gain a concrete understanding of the construction of homepages or the fun of net surfing. So, please click your mouse and discover the exciting homepages that already abound. Learn firsthand from those wonderful pages — it is the best way — how to create your own beautifully designed homepages. Surely it is difficult for us who have little talent and meager experience to create professional-looking pages, but, if the ideas that your mind can conceive really take shape, the whole Internet will benefit through an enlarged network of ideas and art.

Finally, I would like to express my appreciation to Mr. Kazuhiro Hayase, president of Zamza Co., Ltd. for inspiring me and giving me technical advice all throughout my work on this book. I would also like to thank Ms. Honami Morita for help with the layout and Mr. Okuda of Graphic-sha publishing Co., Ltd. Lastly, I want to express my heartfelt thanks to my friends and colleagues at Kinotrope Inc. and to my wife, Sayuri, for her constant support.

Hayashi Sakawa

Chief Editor : Hayase Sakawa (Kinotrope, Inc.)
Text : Hayase Sakawa (Kinotrope, Inc.)
Art Directed : Kazuhiro Hayase (Zamza Co., Ltd.)
Layout : Kazuhiro Hayase, Honami Morita (Studio Pazu)
Homep@ge Chosen : Hayase Sakawa (Kinotrope, Inc.)
Sachiko Miura (Kinotrope, Inc.)
Kazuhiro Hayase
Coordinated : Masahiro Ikuta (Kinotrope, Inc.)
Collaborated : Takako Saito (Zamza Co., Ltd.)
Translation : Rhonda Bagarozzi(AGOSTO)
Atuko Nozawa (AGOSTO)
Sachiko Hiraga (AGOSTO)
DTP Operation : Yuuki Saito (AGOSTO)
Ayako Kawakami (AGOSTO)

Kinotrope, Inc.

3F, Ogawa-Building, 2-41-12,
Tomigaya, Shibuya-ku,
Toukyou-to 150, Japan
Tel: 81-3-5478-8440 / Fax: 81-3-5478-8719
http://www.kinotrope.co.jp
info@kinotrope.co.jp

Zamza Co., Ltd.

2-9-9, Jingumae, Shibuya-ku,
Toukyou-to 160, Japan
Tel: 81-3-5412-8010 / Fax: 81-3-3408-6110
zamza@kinotrope.co.jp